Romans

Grace Revealed

Chester Gross

Copyright © 2012 Chester Gross
All rights reserved.

ISBN: 10:1542862817
ISBN:13:978-1542862813

DEDICATION

To Helen Lynch founder and director of Tell My People Ministries in Dallas, Texas. Thank you for believing in me and urging me to teach the book of Romans. It changed my life forever.

ACKNOWLEGMENTS

All scripture is taken from New Living Translation, copyright © 1996, 2004, 2007, 2013 by Tyndale House Foundation. All rights reserved, unless indicated on the scripture .

CONTENTS

	Acknowledgments	i
1	Covenants	1
2	Introduction	Pg 19
3	The Gospel	Pg 25
4	Gentile Sins	Pg 29
5	Jews and the Law	Pg 37
6	Advantage of Jews	Pg 49
7	Faith of Abraham	Pg 57
8	Peace with God	Pg 71
9	Sin Entered	Pg 83
10	Continue to Sin	Pg 93
11	Conflicting Natures	Pg 107
12	No Condemnation	Pg 123
13	Future Glory	Pg 133
14	Jewish People	Pg 143
15	Salvation for All	Pg 153
16	God's Mercy	Pg 161
17	Transformation	Pg 173
18	Gifts in the Body	Pg 181
19	Really Love People	Pg 193
20	Governing Authority	Pg 203
21	Rules	Pg 211
22	Live in Harmony	Pg 221
23	Final Greetings	Pg 229

FORWARD

This book was written to simplify a complicated topic. This book looks at Romans from a contextual point of view, with an understanding of why Paul wrote this epistle to the churches in Rome and what issues had arisen in the Roman community of faith.

Chapter 1

The Covenants

In the book of Romans, we learn the difference between law and grace. The unspoken background of Romans is about three different covenants. The Abrahamic, the Mosaic and the New Covenant. To the Jewish reader this would be easily understood. They were covenant people and familiar with both the Abrahamic and Mosaic covenants. Now Paul introduces them to the gospel of the New Covenant.

The New and the Mosaic covenants are in stark contrast to each other. Understanding the differences between these covenants is necessary to fully understand

Romans. Paul, who was an expert in the laws of the Mosaic covenant, brings understanding of grace found in the New Covenant.

There are several covenants in scripture, Romans deals with three: The Abrahamic, the Mosaic and the New Covenant. It is important to note that not all covenants are still in effect today, others are still are. For example: God made a covenant with Noah and all of mankind. In this covenant, God promised to never destroy the earth again by flood. HE set the rainbow in the sky as a covenantal sign. When we see the rainbow we know that this covenant is still in effect and we can be assured the world will not be destroyed by water. The Mosaic Covenant as we will see later has been fulfilled through Jesus Christ. This covenant has been removed. The Adamic Covenant is still in effect until we eat from the tree of life at the end of this age, then it will end.

The Bible reveals that God is a covenant making God. The Bible itself is the revelation of several covenants. The Bible is divided into two parts, the Old and the New Testaments or Covenants.

What is a Covenant?

The word Covenant is not heard much today and has lost much of the strength it had in Bible days. Today, with the frequency of petty law suits and the disregard for legal contracts, most people do not understand the true value and responsibility of a covenant relationship.

American Heritage Dictionary
A binding agreement; a compact. A formal sealed agreement or contract. In the Bible, God's promise to the human race.

In the Old Testament, a covenant was the foundation of social order and social relationships. It was the basis for understanding man's relationship with God. The concept of covenants has been used in other cultures as a basis for a wide range of interpersonal and social relationships. A covenant is a treaty between one nation and another.

In the Abrahamic and New covenants their purpose is accomplished at history's end. In the Mosaic covenant the covenant of the Law, God's purpose deals only with the nation of Israel, while the Abrahamic and the New Covenant deal with all people, nations and tribes.

Abrahamic Covenant

This covenant was made with Abraham, (the father of all who believe, and father of the chosen nation of Israel) after the Tower of Babel and the scattering of the sons of Noah in their tongues, families and nations. It involved Abraham, his natural and national seed called Israel and the Messianic seed, Jesus Christ. It includes the coming in of the believing Israelites and Gentiles into the Kingdom of God.

Romans speaks extensively about this covenant and Abrahams faith in God. Abraham's relationship with God was one of faith. Abraham lived more than four hundred years before Moses, therefore he was not subject to the laws which came through Moses. This covenant is vital in understanding Romans because it shows the importance of faith in relationship to righteousness and salvation.

Romans 4:17–22
That is what the Scriptures mean when God told him, "I have made you the father of many nations." This happened because Abraham believed in the God who brings the dead back to life and who creates new things out of nothing. Even when there was no reason for hope, Abraham kept hoping believing that he would become the father of many nations. For God, had said to him, "That's how many descendants you will have!" And Abraham's faith did not weaken, even though, at about 100 years of age, he figured his body was as good as dead and so was Sarah's womb. Abraham never wavered in believing God's promise. In fact, his faith grew stronger, and in this he brought glory to God. He was fully convinced that God can do whatever he promises. And because of Abraham's faith, God counted him as righteous.

Romans 4:11–16
Circumcision was a sign that Abraham already had faith and that God had already accepted him and declared him to be righteous even before he was circumcised. **So Abraham is the spiritual father of those who have faith but have not been circumcised.** They are counted as righteous because of their faith. **And Abraham is also the spiritual father of those who have been circumcised, but only if they have the same kind of faith** Abraham had before he was circumcised. Clearly, God's promise to give the whole earth to Abraham and his descendants was based not on his obedience to God's law, but on a right relationship with God that comes by faith. If God's promise is only for those who obey the law, then faith is not necessary and the promise is pointless. For the law always brings punishment on those who try to obey it. (The only way to avoid breaking the law is to have no law to break!) So the promise is received by faith. It is given as a free gift. And we are all certain to receive it, whether or not we live according to the Law of Moses, if we have faith like Abraham's. For Abraham is the father of all who believe.

The argument is that faith is more important than circumcision and obedience. A right relationship with God only comes through faith, believing the promises of God. Law without faith just brings punishment but does not change the heart nor stop people from sinning.

Abraham was born, lived and died before the Law

ever came into existence. Yet, he was saved, and was spiritual. Neither salvation nor spirituality is contingent upon KEEPING THE LAW, but upon BELIEVING GOD. Abraham became the father of both the Jew's and Gentile's through his offspring Isaac, and Ishmael. This covenant was given to all who would believe whether Jew or Greek. Salvation in both the Old and the New Testaments came through faith. The Old Testament through faith in the ritualistic sacrificial system and the New Testament through faith in the ultimate sacrifice of Jesus the Son of God.

Romans deals with believing Jews who were trying to continue in the Law, and yet still be believers. Paul accuses them of being bewitched and begins to set the proof of faith in Christ. Paul asks them how they received the Spirit, by observing the law or by faith? One cannot obtain righteousness by human efforts. Paul points them back to their Father, Abraham. Consider Abraham: "He believed God and it was credited to him as righteousness."

In the covenant given to Abraham, God promised that all nations would be blessed through him. So, when God announced his plan to Abraham, God revealed the gospel of Jesus Christ to him. When he saw God's plan in the future Abraham believed in Christ before Jesus came. Righteousness was given to him. Abraham looked forward in time and believed in the work of Christ on the cross. Today as believers we look back, having not seen the death and resurrection of Jesus Christ, we believe and receive salvation through our faith the same as Abraham did by believing in Christ by faith before Jesus came.

Galatians 3:8
What's more, the Scriptures looked forward to this time when God would declare the Gentiles to be righteous because of their faith. God proclaimed this good news to Abraham long ago when he said, "All nations will be blessed through you."

We will see much more of the Abrahamic covenant in coming chapters.

Mosaic Covenant

The Mosaic Covenant was made with the chosen nation, Israel, after the Exodus from Egypt at Mt. Sinai. It was made to be a schoolmaster or a teacher to bring the nation of Israel to Jesus Christ, the Savior of the world.

The Mosaic Covenant is the most complicated and most difficult of all covenants to understand. This covenant has intricate details of sacrifice, priesthood, and sanctuary and the complete order of natural and moral laws through Sabbaths and religious festivals and moral codes. Much misunderstanding is found in trying to interpret this covenant. One of the problems is that most people try to combine all the covenants into this one, by making only two covenants an OLD and NEW.

The Mosaic Covenant was Temporary

Again, the law was only a schoolmaster until Christ would come. Once Christ came salvation was bought for all men, and grace was dispensed to mankind. No longer under the schoolmaster of the law, which no one could fulfill except Christ; grace was given to us because Christ the Lamb of God paid for our sins.

Galatians 3:19
Why, then, was the law given? It was given alongside the promise to show people their sins. But the law was designed to last only until the coming of the child who was promised. God gave his law through angels to Moses, who was the mediator between God and the people.

The Mosaic covenant was a temporary covenant given until Christ the seed of Abraham would come. When Jesus provided salvation through his death and resurrection the requirements of the Mosaic Law were fulfilled and removed. Israel still follows it today, at least in part. This is because they rejected Jesus as the Messiah and never enter into the New Covenant.

The Law is Divided into Three Sections

The Mosaic covenant contains more words than any

other covenant given in the Old Testament. It covers several books of the Old Testament. Exodus, Leviticus, Numbers, and Deuteronomy.

Moral Law

This consisted of the ten Commandments written on two tablets of stone given to Moses on Mt. Sinai. The Ten Commandments set forth God's Righteous standard of morality for human conduct in relationship to God and man. Exodus 20; 34:27-28.

Civil Law

This added regulations to the basic principles stated in the Moral Law. This included laws governing society. This would be like our civil laws. It would include such things as what to do with someone caught stealing, or committing murder. Civil law set the punishment for crimes.

Ceremonial Law or Sacrificial Law

This involved the laws governing the sacrifices, priesthood, the temple, and the festivals. These laws provided atonement for the sins of the people. This set specifically how the priests were to prepare and dispense the sacrifices.

Sacrificial Law Removed

We know the sacrificial law has been removed because Jesus as the Lamb of God, laid his life down as a sacrifice for all people. His perfect blood atoned for the sins of the entire world once and for all.

Hebrews 9:11–15
So Christ has now become the High Priest over all the good things that have come. He has entered that greater, more perfect Tabernacle in heaven, which was not made by human hands and is not part of this created world. With his own blood—not the blood of goats and calves—he entered the Most Holy Place once for all time and secured our redemption forever. Under the old system, the blood of goats and bulls and the ashes of a heifer could cleanse people's bodies from ceremonial impurity. Just think how much more the blood of Christ will purify our consciences from sinful deeds so that we can worship the living God. For by the power of the eternal Spirit, Christ offered himself to God as a perfect sacrifice for our sins. That is why he is the one who mediates a new covenant between God and people, so that all who are called can receive the eternal inheritance God has promised them. For Christ died to set them free from the penalty of the sins they had committed under that first covenant.

Civil Law Applies to your own Country

Civil law was the rule that governed society in the nation of Israel. They only applied to the Jewish people and those living within the borders of Israel. Today, we are required to follow the laws of the country in which we live.

Romans 13:1–7
Everyone must submit to governing authorities. For all authority comes from God, and those in positions of authority have been placed there by God. So anyone who rebels against authority is rebelling against what God has instituted, and they will be punished. For the authorities do not strike fear in people who are doing right, but in those who are doing wrong. Would you like to live without fear of the authorities? Do what is right, and they will honor you. The authorities are God's servants, sent for your good. But if you are doing wrong, of course you should be afraid, for they have the power to punish you. They are God's servants, sent for the very purpose of punishing those who do what is wrong. So you must submit to them, not only to avoid punishment, but also to keep a clear conscience. Pay your taxes, too, for these same reasons. For government workers need to be paid. They are serving God in what they do. Give to everyone what you owe them: Pay your taxes and government fees to those who collect them, and give respect and honor to those who are in authority.

Moral Laws has been Modified

The ten commandments make up the basis for the moral law. These commandments are a compass for righteous living. These commandments are broken into two sections.

Relationship to God

1. No other gods before him

2. No graven images to be made or worshipped

3. Not taking the Lord's name in vain

4. Keep the Sabbath day holy to the Lord

Relationship to Man

1. Honor your Father and Mother

2. No murder

3. No adultery

4. No stealing

5. No false witness

6. No coveting

These commandments were to guide us to what is right and honorable before God and to teach us to respect each other.

There were blessings if the people were obedient to the laws of the Mosaic covenant and curses if they disobeyed them. This was a major difference between the Old Testament law and the grace of the New Testament.

The law focused on obedience and punishment based on man's ability to follow the decrees of the law. The New Testament focuses on the grace given to mankind through the sacrifice of Jesus Christ. Jesus did not remove these commandments but changed the way in which they would be obeyed.

Deuteronomy 28:15
"But if you refuse to listen to the LORD your God and do not obey all the commands and decrees I am giving you today, all these curses will come and overwhelm you.

The problem people faced; they were not changed on the inside. They were not regenerated nor had they received a new nature. Therefore, they could only operate in the physical without the Holy Spirit's help to govern their morality.

A New Covenant

The New Covenant was made by Jesus Christ and introduced at the Last Supper. This New Covenant was made for all who would believe in Jesus Christ as the Messiah. This covenant brings the believer into an eternal relationship with God. Jesus came to fulfill the dictates of the Mosaic Law and to release the grace of God. His earthly ministry was a revelation of the Father's Heart; Jesus did only what he saw his Father do. He came to bring eternal redemption to all people.

Entrance into this New Covenant can only be obtained by grace through faith, no longer through circumcision or blind obedience to the law of the Mosaic Covenant. It requires a circumcised heart, a new heart.

Without a new heart and the Holy Spirit mankind could not stop sinning, therefore, they remained under the curse. Obedience was impossible without a renewed spirit and heart.

Jesus shed blood, bought our freedom from a sin nature which kept us from holiness. Now in Jesus we can overcome the sin nature and walk in holiness.

John 3:6
Humans can reproduce only human life, but the Holy Spirit gives birth to spiritual life.

The Holy Spirit has been given to live inside of us to convict us of sin, guide us to live holy. Help us with our weaknesses and lead us daily. Jesus changes the way we follow the moral laws. No longer are we governed by the natural man but by the Spirit of God.

Romans 8:5–6
Those who are dominated by the sinful nature think about sinful things, but those who are controlled by the Holy Spirit think about things that please the Spirit. So, letting your sinful nature control your mind leads to death. But letting the Spirit control your mind leads to life and peace.

Galatians 5:16
So I say, let the Holy Spirit guide your lives. Then you won't be doing what your sinful nature craves.

The Ten Commandments Reduced to Two

Jesus took the four sins we commit against God and said if we would love Him we wouldn't sin against Him. Then he took the six sins we commit against other people and said if we would love people we wouldn't commit sins against them.

Matthew 22:37–40
Jesus replied, " 'You must love the LORD your God with all your heart, all your soul, and all your mind.' This is the first and greatest commandment. A second is equally important: 'Love your neighbor as yourself.' The entire law and all the demands of the prophets are based on these two commandments."

Obedience will never be obtained through coercion or the threat of punishment, therefore, Jesus changed the way we obey the rules. Love produces obedience. Love desires the best for people. Love is kind. Love cares.

The way we fulfill the ten commandments is through love for God and people. Love motivates obedience because no one wants to hurt the person they love. Therefore, love is the key to obedience. Under the Old Testament law the threat of punishment was the motivator to be obedient.

This is in stark contrast with the New Testament principles. With love vs punishment, love wins every time. Remember Paul states in First Corinthians chapter thirteen that love never fails.

What will best motivate us to no longer steal from or murder each other? Love! Love is the motivation that makes obedience possible. Without love our human efforts are just an irritating noise without any real effect.

Three Covenants

Paul addresses the Abrahamic, Mosaic and the New Covenants in the book of Romans. The Abrahamic covenant shows us that without faith the law is worthless. The Mosaic covenant show us that we are now under a new system. The New Covenant shows the way of grace through faith as a better covenant.

As we begin to study Romans we must be reminded of the importance of these covenants and what they each required of mankind and their significance in relationship to righteousness and salvation.

CHESTER GROSS

Chapter 2

Introduction to Romans

The church in Rome was made up of Jews and non-Jews. The church was not founded by Paul, though he knew many leaders there. If Roman Christians could not agree on the meaning of the Gospel, Paul's mission would be compromised. His mission in Romans is to explain the Gospel of salvation through faith in Jesus. He especially highlights that Jesus is the culmination of God's relationship with Israel, and that the Gospel was always meant to spread beyond Israel to non-Jews. Therefore, he focuses so much on key Old Testament themes (Abraham, Torah, circumcision) and on the implications of the Gospel for the Jewish and Gentile relationship.

Romans is the longest letter Paul wrote. It is the only letter he wrote to people he did not know. Paul had never been to Rome when he wrote this letter. Romans is the most theological of his writings, and the most important of his letters, with regard to Christian theology.

The primary purpose of writing to the Christians in Rome was to deal with the relationship between Jew and Gentile with respect to the Gospel of Jesus.

Romans 1:16–17
For I am not ashamed of this Good News about Christ. It is the power of God at work, saving everyone who believes the Jew first and the Gentile. This Good News tells us how God makes us right in his sight. This is accomplished from start to finish by faith. As the Scriptures say, "It is through faith that a righteous person has life."

We do not know who founded the churches in Rome. Nor do we know when these churches were founded. We do know that there were Christ communities in Rome by the mid 40's. In the year 49, Emperor Claudius ordered all Jews expelled from Rome. In 54 Claudius's edict was rescinded. When they returned years later, the Jewish and non-Jewish Christians had a difficult time co-existing. They disagreed about the exact meaning of the Gospel and how exactly to practice the life of following Jesus, especially in religious customs and holy days. Paul's larger dream was to make the church in Rome a staging ground for the

Gospel to spread further west to Spain and beyond.

The letter was most likely written while Paul was in Corinth between 55 and 57 AD. We know it had to be after 54 when the Jewish edict was rescinded. During the years, the Christian Jews were expelled. The Christian Gentiles filled the positions of leadership. So as the Christian Jews began to return to Rome there arose a controversy over adherence to the Jewish law and the roles of leadership.

Paul states his authority of Apostleship to tell the Gentiles what God has done for them and to the Jews who belong to Jesus Christ.

Romans 1:3–5
The Good News is about his Son. In his earthly life, he was born into King David's family line, and he was shown to be the Son of God when he was raised from the dead by the power of the Holy Spirit. He is Jesus Christ our Lord. Through Christ, God has given us the privilege and authority as apostles to tell Gentiles everywhere what God has done for them, so that they will believe and obey him, bringing glory to his name.

Paul begins in the later part of chapter one and into chapter two with an indictment of the Gentile world and the variety of their sins. In chapter two Paul turns his indictment towards the Jews stating that the law (Torah) does not exempt them from judgement. Both Jews and

Gentiles are responsible for the condition of the world and both can only be saved by faith.

Jewish believers were trying to force the Gentile believers; to submit to the law (Torah) to be saved. They believed that because they were God's children, the rituals of the law would give them right standing with God therefore, mixing law and grace together. It is evident that the Jewish believers expected the Gentiles to be circumcised. Paul refutes this belief and shows that both Jew and Gentile are sinners lost without Christ. The law only points the way to faith but cannot save.

Romans 2:17–20
You who call yourselves Jews are relying on God's law, and you boast about your special relationship with him. You know what he wants; you know what is right because you have been taught his law. You are convinced that you are a guide for the blind and a light for people who are lost in darkness. You think you can instruct the ignorant and teach children the ways of God. For you are certain that God's law gives you complete knowledge and truth.

Paul declares one can only be justified by faith in Jesus Christ. Circumcision has value only if you obey all the law, which no one could accomplish. A true Jew is one whose heart is right with God.

Romans 2:25–29
The Jewish ceremony of circumcision has value only if you obey God's law. But if you don't obey God's law, you are no better off than an uncircumcised Gentile. And if the Gentiles obey God's law, won't God declare them to be his own people? In fact, uncircumcised Gentiles who keep God's law will condemn you Jews who are circumcised and possess God's law but don't obey it. For you are not a true Jew just because you were born of Jewish parents or because you have gone through the ceremony of circumcision. No, a true Jew is one whose heart is right with God. And true circumcision is not merely obeying the letter of the law; rather, it is a change of heart produced by the Spirit. And a person with a changed heart seeks praise from God, not from people.

    Paul's theology speaks to the issue dividing the Jewish and Gentile believers, showing all have sinned and fallen short of the Glory of God and need salvation. Paul was one of the greatest theologians of the Jewish law in Israel, once persecuting believing Jews. Now speaking to the differences between grace and the law, he lays out his theology to bring unity to the Christian community in Rome. Paul spends the next several chapters explaining the differences between law and grace through faith, and the work of salvation. Righteousness and holiness are produced through faith in Jesus and a change of heart.

CHESTER GROSS

Chapter 3

The Gospel

Paul sets forth the clearest presentation of the Gospel of Jesus Christ right out of the gate. The Gospel is the issue dividing the Gentile and Jewish converts. Jewish believers want to mix the gospel with the law of the Torah which was devoid of faith and was based on ritual.

The gospel is about God's Son, Period. In the natural, Jesus was born from the line of King David but was the Son of God. He died and was raised from the dead by the power of the Holy Spirit. Jesus Christ is the Messiah!

Romans 1:1–5
This letter is from Paul, a slave of Christ Jesus, chosen by God to be an apostle and sent out to preach his Good News. God promised this Good News long ago through his prophets in the holy Scriptures. The Good News is about his Son. In his earthly life, he was born into King David's family line, and he was shown to be the Son of God when he was raised from the dead by the power of the Holy Spirit. He is Jesus Christ our Lord. Through Christ, God has given us the privilege and authority as apostles to tell Gentiles everywhere what God has done for them, so that they will believe and obey him, bringing glory to his name.

Paul declares his authority as an Apostle to tell Gentiles everywhere about the gospel of Jesus Christ the Son of God so they will believe. Paul begins with the Gentiles but quickly moves to the Jewish people.

Romans 1:6–7
And you are included among those Gentiles who have been called to belong to Jesus Christ. I am writing to all of you in Rome who are loved by God and are called to be his own holy people. May God our Father and the Lord Jesus Christ give you grace and peace.

Paul includes the Jewish and Gentile people which belong to Jesus Christ, both of whom are called to be holy people. The gospel is for all people not just the Jews. Jesus died for all mankind, nations and peoples.

Paul begins his discourse to the Jewish people saying that they are saved by faith in Jesus just the same as the Gentile people. Adherence to the Torah is not enough. Birthright cannot save anyone, nor will circumcision be enough. Being born an Israelite and a follower of the Torah will not save. Only faith in Jesus Christ the Lord, born of a virgin, from the linage of King David, crucified and raised from the dead will save Jew or Gentile. A new era has arrived and new rules apply.

Jesus is the Way, the Truth and the Life. There is salvation in no other name. There is only one road to heaven and his name is Jesus!

Romans 1:16–17
For I am not ashamed of this Good News about Christ. It is the power of God at work, saving everyone who believes the Jew first and also the Gentile. This Good News tells us how God makes us right in his sight. This is accomplished from start to finish by faith. As the Scriptures say, "It is through faith that a righteous person has life."

Paul presents the power of the Gospel and its ability to save, to the Jew first then to the Gentiles. Paul tells us later in Romans that the reason the gospel was given to the Gentiles was because the Jews rejected it. The Gentile branch was grafted into the tree. This gospel saves through faith rather than the law. The law cannot save, Abraham had faith before the law. This emphasis of the gospel changed the way in which righteousness is acquired. Under the Old Testament the adherence to the law brought right standing with God. Now, Jesus, the perfect sacrifice, paid for our righteousness through his blood.

The price is paid, sacrifices are no longer needed. Therefore, a new way through the spirit has come, salvation is given by grace through faith. Faith in Jesus and his sacrifice bring salvation to all men both Jew and Gentile alike.

Chapter 4

Sins of the Gentiles

Romans 1:18–20
But God shows his anger from heaven against all sinful, wicked people who suppress the truth by their wickedness. They know the truth about God because he has made it obvious to them. For ever since the world was created, people have seen the earth and sky. Through everything God made, they can clearly see his invisible qualities his eternal power and divine nature. So, they have no excuse for not knowing God.

Paul begins his argument for the gospel by establishing the sinfulness of all humanity, both Jews and Gentiles. He focuses upon the Gentiles in chapter one and the Jewish people, in chapters two and three. He states that the entire world is guilty of sin and deserves the wrath of God. The first step in presenting the gospel is to convince the hearer that he or she needs it.

Wrath

God's anger is shown to all people who suppress the truth. The term "suppress" refers to people who hold back the gospel from going forward through their sinful and wicked ways.

Anger, which is the strongest of all passions, is a natural impulse. God is very angry and indignant with sin. The older translations use the word, "wrath" which today would make more sense than just the word anger.

Three things are mentioned that provoke God to this intense anger. Godlessness has to do with our attitude toward God. Wickedness has to do with how we behave towards our fellow men. It also has to do with the holding back of the gospel through this ungodly living.

There is no excuse for wickedness and sinful living since God has made himself obvious to all mankind. The earth, sky and everything God has made clearly reveals God's eternal power and divine nature so no one has an excuse for not knowing God.

Romans 1:21–23
Yes, they knew God, but they wouldn't worship him as God or even give him thanks. And they began to think up foolish ideas of what God was like. Thus, their minds became dark and confused. Claiming to be wise, they instead became utter fools. And instead of worshiping the glorious, ever-living God, they worshiped idols made to look like mere people and birds and animals and reptiles.

Every culture in the world has a supreme being or god. Many cultures have many gods yet they still have one that is above all the rest. The Greeks had Zeus, the Romans, Jupiter and the Egyptians had Ra, gods were seen through nature and each god had a different purpose. So, all men had a clear picture of God yet chose not to worship him. They thought up foolish ideas of what God was like. India alone has hundreds of god's. Some believe India has over 330 million gods.

Abandoned to Shameful Things

Romans 1:24–25
So, God abandoned them to do whatever shameful things their hearts desired. As a result, they did vile and degrading things with each other's bodies. They traded the truth about God for a lie. So they worshiped and served the things God created instead of the Creator himself, who is worthy of eternal praise! Amen.

These ideas are ridiculous and foolish. God, through their darkened minds, gave them over to do whatever their hearts desired. God allowed men, in their foolishness, to follow their most wicked desires leading them to un-natural sexual relations. They served created things instead of the creator of the universe and brought God to the level of mankind. They believed the lie.

The witness to God in nature is so clear and so constant that ignoring it is indefensible. Their condemnation is based not on their rejecting Christ of whom they have not heard, but on their sinning against the light they had.

Romans 1:26–27
That is why God abandoned them to their shameful desires. Even the women turned against the natural way to have sex and instead indulged in sex with each other. And the men, instead of having normal sexual relations with women, burned with lust for each other. Men did shameful things with other men, and as a result of this sin, they suffered within themselves the penalty they deserved.

The Greek for 'shameful' is *atimias* which means, without honor. When men refuse to honor God, God gives them over to lusts that are without honor.

It is always uncomfortable to discuss sexual sins,

especially homosexuality but scripture is very clear what God's opinion is here in Romans. I don't see how the apostle could make it any clearer than he does here. For men to be involved sexually with men is dishonorable. It involves the committing of indecent acts which lead to punishment. This was the sin for which God destroyed Sodom and Gomorrah in the book of Genesis. Paul continues adding that women are doing the same thing.

Romans 1:27
And the men, instead of having normal sexual relations with women, burned with lust for each other. Men did shameful things with other men, and as a result of this sin, they suffered within themselves the penalty they deserved.

The phrase "they suffered within themselves", here refers to the natural result of their sin which pays them back for what they have done. Nature will pay them back for their dishonor to God. God's divine order has decreed payback for sin.

Sins of the Gentiles

Romans 1:28–32
Since they thought it foolish to acknowledge God, he abandoned them to their foolish thinking and let them do things that should never be done. Their lives became full of every kind of wickedness, sin, greed, hate, envy,

murder, quarreling, deception, malicious behavior, and gossip. They are backstabbers, haters of God, insolent, proud, and boastful. They invent new ways of sinning, and they disobey their parents. They refuse to understand, break their promises, are heartless, and have no mercy. They know God's justice requires that those who do these things deserve to die, yet they do them anyway. Worse yet, they encourage others to do them, too.

The abandonment of God led to every kind of wickedness. Paul names nine wicked behaviors which follow those who refuse to acknowledge God. Wickedness refers to an unrighteous life. Sin is translated wickedness, which means to be a lawbreaker or a transgressor. Greed is to desire more but cannot be satisfied, it is to covet what other people have.

Hate in not a term we would expect. It is moral depravity or bad character. Someone devoid of morals and contaminated by sin. Envy is the feeling of displeasure produced by witnessing or hearing of the advantage or prosperity of others; the sense of evil always attaches itself to this word. Envy always produces extreme resentment toward other people.

Murder is the taking of a life through deliberate sinful and moral actions. Quarreling is a heated argument which creates strife, contention and fighting. Deception is to use bait like you would to catch a fish. It is deceiving through fraud.

Malicious behavior is to have a bad attitude which causes bad behavior. It also has the intention of doing harm to others. Gossip is a whisperer, someone who repeats information with the purpose of hurting the person they are talking about.

Next, Paul describes them as backstabbers, haters of God, insolent, proud and boastful. A backstabber is someone who speaks evil of people with the intent to cause damage to their reputation. They hate God and are insolent which is to be despiteful in a violent manner. They are proud and arrogant showing themselves to be above everyone else. They are boastful always bragging about themselves.

These people invent new ways of sinning and disobey their parents. This is interesting that it is listed in the list of sins. They are unwilling to receive any form of correction from their parents leading them to these sins.

Romans 1:31–32
They refuse to understand, break their promises, are heartless, and have no mercy. They know God's justice requires that those who do these things deserve to die, yet they do them anyway. Worse yet, they encourage others to do them, too.

They will not listen to reason, they do not keep their word and are heartless, which is devoid of natural affection for their family. They are merciless and do not have compassion for the hurting. They know God will judge someday but they don't care. They continue to encourage others to live the same way they do.

This is a long list of wicked sins which the Gentiles are guilty of. Paul states his case in the most drastic way possible. I can image the Jews reading this and agreeing thinking they are immune to these sins. But Paul is setting them up for the fall. These converted Jews thought they were superior to the Gentiles because they were from the seed of Abraham and the covenant of God. They did not commit these sins so they were exempt from this line of thinking, or so they thought.

Paul nails his thesis on the wall in the next chapter. He includes them in these sins and lets them know in no uncertain terms that they are guilty of the same sins and deserve the same anger from God as the Gentiles.

Chapter 5

Jews and the Law

Paul finished chapter one with a long list of sins which were common to the Gentile pagans. I would assume that at this point of his writing the Jewish believers are shouting Amen! Yes, brother Paul, we are God's chosen people those Gentiles are dogs and pagans. We are the circumcised children of God through the line of Abraham. We are superior because we are covenant partners with God, and follow the law.

They believed they followed the law even though they were incapable of obeying it in its entirety which made them as guilty of sin as the Gentiles. They thought they could condemn the Gentile people because of this long list of sins, yet Paul declares they are without excuse for they commit the same sins. Therefore, they should not pass judgment for God's anger is against all who sin both Jew and Gentile.

Romans 2:1–3
You may think you can condemn such people, but you are just as bad, and you have no excuse! When you say they are wicked and should be punished, you are condemning yourself, for you who judge others do these very same things. And we know that God, in his justice, will punish anyone who does such things. Since you judge others for doing these things, why do you think you can avoid God's judgment when you do the same things?

In chapter one we learned that Gentiles, who rejected the revelation of God in nature, were without excuse (1:20). Now we learn that Jews who pass judgment on their pagan neighbors have "no excuse" (2:1). In the very act of condemning others, they automatically condemned themselves because they were guilty of doing the same things.

Jesus made it clear that if we judge others we will be judged in return. Whatever we sow is what we will reap. Judgment and condemnation will produce after their own kind. Forgiving will ensure we are forgiven. These are principles of the Kingdom of God.

Luke 6:37
"Do not judge others, and you will not be judged. Do not condemn others, or it will all come back against you. Forgive others, and you will be forgiven.

Galatians 6:7
Don't be misled you cannot mock the justice of God. You will always harvest what you plant.

Tolerance of God

Romans 2:4
Don't you see how wonderfully kind, tolerant, and patient God is with you? Does this mean nothing to you? Can't you see that his kindness is intended to turn you from your sin?

These next words seem out of place after what was just discussed. Paul listed numerous sins in which both Jew and Gentile were guilty of committing. He then tells them not to be quick to judge or they would be judged, for they were sinning just the same. Now he asks the question: "isn't God wonderfully kind, tolerant and patient with you?"

By not exacting His divine penalty on sinful humanity immediately, God is displaying the riches of His kindness, which is benevolence in action. God is also tolerant, and patient. God's purpose is to lead people toward repentance so they will return to Him through His wonderful kindness. Paul states in chapter three that Jesus was given as the sacrifice for sin so that people might be made right with God. The sacrifice of Jesus shows that God was fair and did not punish those who sinned.

Romans 3:25
For God presented Jesus as the sacrifice for sin. People are made right with God when they believe that Jesus sacrificed his life, shedding his blood. This sacrifice shows that God was being fair when he held back and did not punish those who sinned in times past.

Gods kindness, (benevolence in action) withheld His wrath and judgment providing righteousness towards those who sinned. It is through the kindness of God that we are drawn to repentance. Tolerance is to delay punishment, to offer opportunity to repent. Along with tolerance God was patience with us to give ample time for us to come to him. Let's remember that under the Mosaic law obedience was encouraged through the fear of punishment. This is a new thought to the Jewish believers that God's kindness is intended to turn people from sin.

Can you imagine what the Jewish believers are thinking? First Paul blasts them with the fact that they are just as sinful as the Gentiles, this was overwhelming at the least. Then to reveal that it is through kindness and patience that people are drawn to a repentant heart. I don't believe they were expecting this from the Paul, whom they knew was an expert in the Jewish law.

Righteous Judgment

Romans 2:5–11
But because you are stubborn and refuse to turn from your sin, you are storing up terrible punishment for yourself. For a day of anger is coming, when God's righteous judgment will be revealed. He will judge everyone according to what they have done. He will give eternal life to those who keep on doing good, seeking after the glory and honor and immortality that God offers. But he will pour out his anger and wrath on those who live for themselves, who refuse to obey the truth and instead live lives of wickedness. There will be trouble and calamity for everyone who keeps on doing what is evil—for the Jew first and also for the Gentile. But there will be glory and honor and peace from God for all who do good—for the Jew first and also for the Gentile. For God does not show favoritism.

Their stubborn and uncaring attitude towards sin is storing up the punishment they deserve. This punishment is not coming now but later when God's righteousness will be revealed.

This was another new thought to these Jewish believers. Judgment under the law brought punishment right away in this life. Now it is being stored up for a day of judgment later.

EVERYONE is judged according to what they have done. There will be no favoritism towards either Jew or Gentile. Everyone will be judged according to the life they are living. Eternal life will be given to those who are persistent in doing good. God's wrath will be poured out on Jew and Gentile peoples who live for themselves and live in wickedness.

Wickedness is to live in an unrighteous state. Unrighteousness refers to all people who do not receive the gospel of Jesus Christ and continue to live without God.

All who consistently live this way will find trouble and calamity. Trouble means to be afflicted or burdened in one's spirit, while calamity is the distress caused by the burden in one's spirit.

This judgment will come to the Jew first because they had the law and knew what God expected from them and yet did not obey. So, judgment would be given to them before the Gentiles. Again, this must be overwhelming to them because they are certain, that because of their heritage and covenant with God they are superior to all other peoples. Paul clearly asserts that God will not favor them over the Gentiles.

When the Gentiles sin, destruction follows. Destruction here does not mean to annihilate but to bring to ruin. The Gentiles will suffer the loss of wellbeing and the joy of salvation if they follow their own ways. The Jews will be judged by the very law for which they are boasting. Merely quoting the law or listening to it will not make them right in God's eyes, they must obey it completely. Even the Gentiles, when they do what is right show that the law of God is written on their hearts. They demonstrate it by their own conscience which convicts them of their sin. Finally, a day is coming in which God will judge everyone's secret life through Jesus Christ.

Jews and the Law

Romans 2:17–24
You who call yourselves Jews are relying on God's law, and you boast about your special relationship with him. You know what he wants; you know what is right because you have been taught his law. You are convinced that you are a guide for the blind and a light for people who are lost in darkness. You think you can instruct the ignorant and teach children the ways of God. For you are certain that God's law gives you complete knowledge and truth. Well then, if you teach others, why don't you teach yourself? You tell others not to steal, but do you steal? You say it is wrong to commit adultery, but do you commit adultery? You condemn idolatry, but do you use items stolen from pagan temples? You are so proud of knowing the law, but

you dishonor God by breaking it. No wonder the Scriptures say, "The Gentiles blaspheme the name of God because of you."

Paul addressed his listeners directly: "Now you, if you call yourself a Jew" and of course they did! To be a member of the Jewish race was to enjoy certain religious advantages over other nations. Gradually, however, privilege gave birth to self-righteousness. Paul understood the sentiments of those to whom he wrote because prior to conversion he himself was among those who were the most zealous for their Jewish heritage (Gal 1:14).

They relied on the law. God had revealed himself to Israel through Moses and laid out his expectations for them. Their national identity was bound up with the Mosaic laws. They boasted of their unique relationship with God. He was theirs and theirs alone. No other nation had been so blessed. God was the father of Israel. Another advantage for the Jews was their knowledge of the will of God. God had clearly revealed to the nation what he expected of them.

The Jewish believers saw themselves superior to the Gentiles because they had the law and a special relationship with God. Yet their relationship was obtained through Abraham the father of their nation. They were only covenant people through physical circumcision and obedience to the law. Although they were circumcised they could not obey the law because they did not have a new heart which could only come through faith in Christ.

They were convinced because of their superiority to the Gentiles that they should be their guides, and that they should teach and instruct them in the ways of God. Paul condemns them asking, "if you teach others why don't you teach yourself?" "Do you steal or commit adultery?" They were proud they knew the law, yet they constantly broke the law which deserved the same punishment as the Gentiles.

The Value of Circumcision

Romans 2:25–29
The Jewish ceremony of circumcision has value only if you obey God's law. But if you don't obey God's law, you are no better off than an uncircumcised Gentile. And if the Gentiles obey God's law, won't God declare them to be his own people? In fact, uncircumcised Gentiles who keep God's law will condemn you Jews who are circumcised and possess God's law but don't obey it. For you are not a true Jew just because you were born of Jewish parents or because you have gone through the ceremony of circumcision. No, a true Jew is one whose heart is right with God. And true circumcision is not merely obeying the letter of the law; rather, it is a change of heart produced by the Spirit. And a person with a changed heart seeks praise from God, not from people.

Circumcision identified the Jewish people as the children of God, but without obedience to the law they were still in their sin. So, circumcision only had value if the law was obeyed. The Gentiles were better off if they kept the law than the Jews who were circumcised.

Galatians 5:2–4
Listen! I, Paul, tell you this: If you are counting on circumcision to make you right with God, then Christ will be of no benefit to you. I'll say it again. If you are trying to find favor with God by being circumcised, you must obey every regulation in the whole law of Moses. For if you are trying to make yourselves right with God by keeping the law, you have been cut off from Christ! You have fallen away from God's grace.

In this new covenant, circumcision did not have the same value as before. A true Jew was someone whose heart was right with God. True circumcision was a changed heart not just a physical procedure.

Galatians makes it clear that if they were counting on circumcision to make them right with God then Jesus had no benefit for them. If they try to make themselves right with God by the law they are cut off from Christ and God's grace.

Jesus is the only person to ever keep the entire law. During the twenty-five hundred years, the law was in effect, no one could keep it all. The law was related to man's attempts for righteousness without Christ. It was self-promotion and works of the flesh. Through faith in Jesus Christ, obedience to the law was no longer required salvation in the New Covenant is received by grace through faith in Jesus Christ.

Ephesians 2:8–9
God saved you by his grace when you believed. And you can't take credit for this; it is a gift from God. Salvation is not a reward for the good things we have done, so none of us can boast about it.

Jews and Gentiles are now one People

Ephesians 2:11–18
Don't forget that you Gentiles used to be outsiders. You were called "uncircumcised heathens" by the Jews, who were proud of their circumcision, even though it affected only their bodies and not their hearts. In those days you were living apart from Christ. You were excluded from citizenship among the people of Israel, and you did not know the covenant promises God had made to them. You lived in this world without God and without hope. But now you have been united with Christ Jesus. Once you were far away from God, but now you have been brought near to him through the blood of Christ. For Christ himself has brought peace to us. He united Jews and Gentiles into one people when, in his own body on the cross, he broke down

the wall of hostility that separated us. He did this by ending the system of law with its commandments and regulations. He made peace between Jews and Gentiles by creating in himself one new people from the two groups. Together as one body, Christ reconciled both groups to God by means of his death on the cross, and our hostility toward each other was put to death. He brought this Good News of peace to you Gentiles who were far away from him, and peace to the Jews who were near. Now all of us can come to the Father through the same Holy Spirit because of what Christ has done for us.

The Jews and the Gentiles are now one people through the blood of Jesus Christ. The hostility between the Jews and Gentiles was caused by the law, therefore God removed it, creating peace for both peoples who are now one body in Christ.

Chapter 6

What is the Advantage of being a Jew

Romans 3:1–2
Then what's the advantage of being a Jew? Is there any value in the ceremony of circumcision? Yes, there are great benefits! First of all, the Jews were entrusted with the whole revelation of God.

The advantage was the Jews were entrusted with the oracles of God. In a Jewish context 'oracles' can hardly mean anything other than Scripture, and it was to the Jews that the divine speech recorded in Scripture was given. We must remember that the law was the word of God given to Israel through Moses on Mount Sinai. Later in the chapter Paul tells us why the law was given.

Next Paul returns to his brusque language toward the Jews. They no longer had any position in which they were superior to the Gentiles for they sinned just as much as the Gentiles and were also without excuse.

Romans 3:9–12
Well then, should we conclude that we Jews are better than others? No, not at all, for we have already shown that all people, whether Jews or Gentiles, are under the power of sin. As the Scriptures say,

> "No one is righteous
>   not even one.
> No one is truly wise;
>   no one is seeking God.
> All have turned away;
>   all have become useless.
> No one does good,
>   not a single one."

The case is made. The Jews are not better than the Gentiles. All people are under the power of sin and no one is righteous. Only faith in Jesus can change the problem all men face.

The Purpose of the Law

Romans 3:19–20
Obviously, the law applies to those to whom it was given, for its purpose is to keep people from having excuses, and to show that the entire world is guilty before God. For no one can ever be made right with God by doing what the law commands. The law simply shows us how sinful we are.

The law applies only to the Jewish people, it was never given to the Gentiles. No one can ever be made right with God by obeying the law. So, even the Jews to whom the law was given had no excuse for their sin. The law was given to show all people how sinful they are. The law only reveals our sin it does not make us righteous.

Galatians 3:11-14
Clearly no one is justified before God by the law, because, "The righteous will live by faith." The law is not based on faith; on the contrary, "The man who does these things will live by them." Christ redeemed us from the curse of the law by becoming a curse for us, for it is written: "Cursed is everyone who is hung on a tree." He redeemed us in order that the blessing given to Abraham might come to the Gentiles through Christ Jesus, so that by faith we might receive the promise of the Spirit.

The law is based on the curse of Adam, not faith in Jesus Christ. The law set the standard by which punishment is determined creating a curse. Jesus through his death and resurrection redeemed us from the curse created by the law.

Why was the law added? The law was only given until the seed would come. We know that the seed is Jesus Christ. Therefore, the law was not meant to govern us for all time. It had its purpose, but when Jesus came and introduced the New Covenant there was no more need for the Old Covenant law.

Romans 5:20-21
The law was added so that the trespass might increase. But where sin increased, grace increased all the more, so that, just as sin reigned in death, so also grace might reign through righteousness to bring eternal life through Jesus Christ our Lord.

The law was a teacher put in charge to lead us to Christ. Now that faith has come, we no longer are to live under the law. This is one of the areas the church has missed. The church is still trying to mix both covenants.

A New Way of Righteousness

Romans 3:21–22
But now God has shown us a way to be made right with him without keeping the requirements of the law, as was promised in the writings of Moses and the prophets long ago. We are made right with God by placing our faith in

Jesus Christ. And this is true for everyone who believes, no matter who we are.

Paul has spent the better part of three chapters slamming the self-righteousness of the Jews. Now he lays out the new way of righteousness. Legalism to the law is no longer the means to be right with God. Jesus has changed everything. A new way has come by placing our faith in Jesus Christ.

Romans 3:23–26
For everyone has sinned; we all fall short of God's glorious standard. Yet God freely and graciously declares that we are righteous. He did this through Christ Jesus when he freed us from the penalty for our sins. For God presented Jesus as the sacrifice for sin. People are made right with God when they believe that Jesus sacrificed his life, shedding his blood. This sacrifice shows that God was being fair when he held back and did not punish those who sinned in times past, for he was looking ahead and including them in what he would do in this present time. God did this to demonstrate his righteousness, for he himself is fair and just, and he declares sinners to be right in his sight when they believe in Jesus.

Here is the famous verse of Christendom. "All of them have sinned and fallen short of the grace of God." No one was righteous or good, all were sinners. Now Paul puts them all on equal ground. Jewish and Gentile believers are all sinners and all in need of salvation.

Now we are given righteousness freely and released from our sins by the shedding of Jesus blood. Jesus became the sacrifice for sin shedding His blood. Right standing with God has changed forever. All people are made right with God by believing in Jesus and his sacrifice. There is no longer a need for the law to make us righteous.

Romans 3:27–31
Can we boast, then, that we have done anything to be accepted by God? No, because our acquittal is not based on obeying the law. It is based on faith. So, we are made right with God through faith and not by obeying the law. After all, is God the God of the Jews only? Isn't he also the God of the Gentiles? Of course he is. There is only one God, and he makes people right with himself only by faith, whether they are Jews or Gentiles. Well then, if we emphasize faith, does this mean that we can forget about the law? Of course not! In fact, only when we have faith do we truly fulfill the law.

Freedom from the law is not based on our obedience, rather it is through our faith. God makes all people right with himself ONLY by faith.

Romans 3:31
Well then, if we emphasize faith, does this mean that we can forget about the law? Of course not! In fact, only when

we have faith do we truly fulfill the law.

Paul presented his case that God declares people righteous on the principle of faith instead of works. Man's works no longer are the means to right standing with God. So why did God give the law in the first place?

Galatians 3:19
Why, then, was the law given? It was given alongside the promise to show people their sins. But the law was designed to last only until the coming of the child who was promised. God gave his law through angels to Moses, who was the mediator between God and the people.

Galatians 3:23–25
Before the way of faith in Christ was available to us, we were placed under guard by the law. We were kept in protective custody, so to speak, until the way of faith was revealed. Let me put it another way. The law was our guardian until Christ came; it protected us until we could be made right with God through faith. And now that the way of faith has come, we no longer need the law as our guardian.

Until Christ came as the object of faith, the law had to act as a child-custodian for us. The law acted as an outward check on desires, making the consciousness of sin more acute. It further emphasized that man is himself unable to deal with sin, guiding him to Christ.

The moral law shows what man ought to do, and he learns his inability to do it. The ceremonial law tried, using animal sacrifices, to compensate for this inability. Dead animals, however, did not satisfy the needs of living men for forgiveness. They pointed to a perfect sacrifice, the fulfillment of all sacrifices, which was Jesus.

The judicial law shows the doom man deserves, and leads him to righteousness and peace in Christ. The message of the Old Testament, that men are doomed for their sin, is important because without it the New Testament message of grace and salvation would have no meaning. After faith came, we are no longer under a schoolmaster. Christ has set us free!

Chapter 7

Faith of Abraham

Romans 4:1–3
Abraham was, humanly speaking, the founder of our Jewish nation. What did he discover about being made right with God? If his good deeds had made him acceptable to God, he would have had something to boast about. But that was not God's way. For the Scriptures tell us, "Abraham believed God, and God counted him as righteous because of his faith."

Paul, the Apostle, goes right back to the beginning of it all, Abraham! What did he discover about this matter? Abraham is the father of Israel; the first man to have a covenant with God regarding the nation of Israel. The Messiah would come from the seed of Abraham. All of Israel's history begins with Abraham.

If Abraham was made right with God through his good works then he could not have boasted to God concerning it. The question is asked, "what does scripture have to say about this?"

Genesis 15:2–6
But Abram replied, "O Sovereign Lord, what good are all your blessings when I don't even have a son? Since you've given me no children, Eliezer of Damascus, a servant in my household, will inherit all my wealth. You have given me no descendants of my own, so one of my servants will be my heir." Then the Lord said to him, "No, your servant will not be your heir, for you will have a son of your own who will be your heir." Then the Lord took Abram outside and said to him, "Look up into the sky and count the stars if you can. That's how many descendants you will have!" **And Abram believed the Lord, and the Lord counted him as righteous because of his faith.**

Scripture declares that Abraham's righteousness came from his faith not his works. God promised Abraham a son in his old age. Abraham put his faith in God's word. He believed if God promised then it would happen.

Romans 4:4–5
When people work, their wages are not a gift, but something they have earned. But people are counted as righteous, not because of their work, but because of their faith in God who forgives sinners.

Payment for work is not a gift but something earned. Righteousness cannot be worked for or earned. Right standing with God comes because of faith in God's forgiveness through Jesus sacrifice. The Jewish believers had focused on the law for so long they most likely had never considered Abraham's faith.

Abraham lived four hundred and thirty years before Moses. The law came through Moses to the people of Israel after they fled the captivity of Egypt. At the time Abraham lived, the law did not exist. His righteousness was not because he did everything right. He allowed two different kings to take his wife. If God had not intervened, he would have lost Sarah. His righteousness was given to him because of his faith in God.

John 1:17
For the law was given through Moses, but God's unfailing love and faithfulness came through Jesus Christ.

For Jews and Gentiles

Romans 4:9–10

Now, is this blessing only for the Jews, or is it also for uncircumcised Gentiles? Well, we have been saying that Abraham was counted as righteous by God because of his faith. But how did this happen? Was he counted as righteous only after he was circumcised, or was it before he was circumcised? Clearly, God accepted Abraham before he was circumcised!

The case of circumcision was made quite clearly in chapter two verse twenty-eight. "For you are not a true Jew just because you were born of Jewish parents or because you have gone through the ceremony of circumcision. No, a true Jew is one whose heart is right with God."

Paul again raised the question of the Jews' position. The way the question is worded in the Greek suggests the answer, that **this blessedness** is **for the uncircumcised** (Gentiles) as well as **for the circumcised** (Jews). But in response Paul turned again to the example of Abraham.

He repeated a scriptural declaration that Abraham was declared righteous based on his faith. Then Paul asked whether Abraham's justification occurred before or after he was circumcised. Answering his own question, Paul stated, it was not after, but before!

Abraham's age when he was declared righteous (Gen.

15:6) is not stated. But later when Hagar bore him Ishmael, he was eighty-six (Gen. 16:16). After that, God instructed Abraham to perform the rite of circumcision on all his male descendants as a sign of God's covenant with him; this was done when Abraham was ninety-nine (Gen. 17:24). Therefore, the circumcision of Abraham followed his justification by faith by more than thirteen years.

Romans 4:11–12
Circumcision was a sign that Abraham already had faith and that God had already accepted him and declared him to be righteous even before he was circumcised. So Abraham is the spiritual father of those who have faith but have not been circumcised. They are counted as righteous because of their faith. And Abraham is also the spiritual father of those who have been circumcised, but only if they have the same kind of faith Abraham had before he was circumcised.

Abraham's circumcision was the physical sign of his righteousness through faith before he was circumcised. God's purpose was that Abraham would be the father of all who believed which included the uncircumcised Gentiles and the circumcised Jews.

The rite of circumcision which the Jews relied on for salvation did not make them right before God. Paul asserts that righteousness can only be aquired through faith.

The Law is not Based on Faith

Romans 4:13–15
Clearly, God's promise to give the whole earth to Abraham and his descendants was based not on his obedience to God's law, but on a right relationship with God that comes by faith. If God's promise is only for those who obey the law, then faith is not necessary and the promise is pointless. For the law always brings punishment on those who try to obey it. (The only way to avoid breaking the law is to have no law to break!)

This is strong language to the Jewish readers. If God's promise is only for those who obey the law, then faith is not necessary and the promise is pointless. If righteousness comes through our own obedience to the law, then Jesus died for nothing and the promise is worthless.

Galatians 5:2–4
Listen! I, Paul, tell you this: If you are counting on circumcision to make you right with God, then Christ will be of no benefit to you. I'll say it again. If you are trying to find favor with God by being circumcised, you must obey every regulation in the whole law of Moses. For if you are trying to make yourselves right with God by keeping the law, you have been cut off from Christ! You have fallen away from God's grace.

I can imagine the Jews freaking out right now. They have lived all their lives believing they were right with God because they were the children of God through circumcision and adherence to the law. Now Paul destroys everything they have ever known.

Favor with God cannot be obtained through circumcision. The law requires that every regulation be obeyed, which no one could accomplish. Now they are being told that their faith in Jesus Christ is pointless if they are made right with God through the law. In fact, they would be cut off from Christ himself and would lose grace.

Grace is the undeserved favor from God apart from our obedience and faithfulness to the law. It is a gift from God given to all who believe.

Romans 5:16
And the result of God's gracious gift is very different from the result of that one man's sin. For Adam's sin led to condemnation, but God's free gift leads to our being made right with God, even though we are guilty of many sins.

For the law always brings punishment upon those who try to obey it. The only way to avoid breaking the law is to have no law to break! The law simply shows us how sinful we are but cannot make us right with God.

The Law brings wrath (the Law keeps on producing

wrath) because of disobedience. No one can keep the Law fully; therefore God, in wrath against sin, judges those who disobey.

Paul then stated a simple principle: Where there is no law, there is no sin. A person may still be sinning in his action, but if there is no command prohibiting it, his action cannot be considered sinful. Without drawing a line in the sand and issuing the command not to cross it, how can one be punished for crossing where the line could have been? There is no line therefore there can be no punishment.

Romans 3:19–20
Obviously, the law applies to those to whom it was given, for its purpose is to keep people from having excuses, and to show that the entire world is guilty before God. For no one can ever be made right with God by doing what the law commands. The law simply shows us how sinful we are.

The covenant of the law was complicated and difficult to follow. Sacrifices had to be made to appease the anger of God. Obedience to the rules governed the blessings of God. The law was never meant to bring salvation to mankind but to show their need for God. Jesus came as the final sacrifice to redeem all mankind from the sin of Adam. (We will talk more about Adam in chapter five.) Now like Abraham we are made right with God through our faith in Jesus Christ and what he has done, not our own attempts at doing what is right.

Promise is Received by Faith

Romans 4:16–19
So the promise is received by faith. It is given as a free gift. And we are all certain to receive it, whether or not we live according to the law of Moses, if we have faith like Abraham's. For Abraham is the father of all who believe. That is what the Scriptures mean when God told him, "I have made you the father of many nations." This happened because Abraham believed in the God who brings the dead back to life and who creates new things out of nothing. Even when there was no reason for hope, Abraham kept hoping believing that he would become the father of many nations. For God had said to him, "That's how many descendants you will have!" And Abraham's faith did not weaken, even though, at about 100 years of age, he figured his body was as good as dead and so was Sarah's womb.

Though humanly there was no hope of ever having a child, the old patriarch believed God's Word. Against all hope, Abraham believed. God honored his faith, and he became the father (ancestor) of many nations. This was in accord with God's promise.

Abraham, without weakening in his faith, faced the

fact that his body was as good as dead (a reference to the patriarch's advanced age of one hundred (Gen. 17:17; 21:5). Abraham also considered carefully that Sarah's womb was also dead. She was unable to conceive a child, as had been demonstrated through their life together and as was certainly true for her at age ninety (Gen. 17:17).

Romans 4:20–25
Abraham never wavered in believing God's promise. In fact, his faith grew stronger, and in this he brought glory to God. He was fully convinced that God is able to do whatever he promises. And because of Abraham's faith, God counted him as righteous. And when God counted him as righteous, it wasn't just for Abraham's benefit. It was recorded for our benefit, too, assuring us that God will also count us as righteous if we believe in him, the one who raised Jesus our Lord from the dead. He was handed over to die because of our sins, and he was raised to life to make us right with God.

Despite the humanly impossible situation, Abraham did not waver through unbelief. Abraham was strengthened in his faith and empowered by means of faith. God, responding to Abraham's faith, empowered him and Sarah physically to generate the child of promise. Also, Abraham gave glory to God. He praised God by exalting or exclaiming God's attributes. Abraham was fully persuaded that God had power (spiritual ability) to do what He had promised.

Paul concluded his illustration about Abraham by saying, therefore it was credited to him as righteousness. Abraham believed in the God who brings the dead back to life and who creates new things out of nothing. Therefore, he believed God could give Sarah and him a son in old age.

Romans 4:23–25
And when God counted him as righteous, it wasn't just for Abraham's benefit. It was recorded for our benefit, too, assuring us that God will also count us as righteous if we believe in him, the one who raised Jesus our Lord from the dead. He was handed over to die because of our sins, and he was raised to life to make us right with God.

If we believe the same way Abraham believed, we will also be counted as righteous. Jesus was handed over to die for our sins and was raised to life to make us right with God.

In chapters one through three Paul deals with the superiority of the Jews who believed they were better than the Gentiles based on circumcision and the covenant of the law. All Jews and Gentiles have sinned and fallen short of the expectation of God, no one is righteous. Paul brings them back to their own history through Abraham. How did Abraham become righteous? Was he made righteous before or after the law? The real children of Abraham are those who put their faith in God.

Galatians 3:6–7
In the same way, "Abraham believed God, and God counted him as righteous because of his faith." The real children of Abraham, then, are those who put their faith in God.

The Gospel Preached to Abraham

Galatians 3:8–9
What's more, the Scriptures looked forward to this time when God would declare the Gentiles to be righteous because of their faith. God proclaimed this good news to Abraham long ago when he said, "All nations will be blessed through you." So all who put their faith in Christ share the same blessing Abraham received because of his faith.

I believe Abraham was the first person to become "born again," as we know it today. Abraham took Isaac to the mountain of God with the intent to sacrifice him as a burnt offering to God. This story is the picture of God the Father giving His son Jesus to the world as the lamb of God. Abraham believed that God would raise Isaac from the dead. I believe this is where God preached the gospel of Jesus Christ to Abraham.

Abraham believed in what Jesus would do in the future on the cross. Looking to the future, he had faith that what God promised he would do. Righteousness was then credited to him. Why was it credited? Jesus had not died yet, Abraham had righteousness credited to him because of his faith.

Today, you and I have been made righteous by looking back through time and believing in what Jesus did in the past. By faith we are given righteousness. Neither Abraham, or any of us have seen Jesus die on the cross. Abraham looked forward, we look back and by faith we are made righteous. Abraham became the father of all who believe both Jew and Gentile.

Romans 4:16–17
So the promise is received by faith. It is given as a free gift. And we are all certain to receive it, whether or not we live according to the law of Moses, if we have faith like Abraham's. For Abraham is the father of all who believe. That is what the Scriptures mean when God told him, "I have made you the father of many nations." This happened because Abraham believed in the God who brings the dead back to life and who creates new things out of nothing.

CHESTER GROSS

Chapter 8

Peace with God

Romans 5:1–2
Therefore, since we have been made right in God's sight by faith, we have peace with God because of what Jesus Christ our Lord has done for us. Because of our faith, Christ has brought us into this place of undeserved privilege where we now stand, and we confidently and joyfully look forward to sharing God's glory.

For three and a half chapters Paul has dealt with righteousness, judgement, and justification. He can now focus on justification, the result of God's gracious act of redemption in Jesus Christ, and proceed to consider some of its consequences.

The first result of justification is peace with God. Indeed, to say that we have peace with God is hardly more than to say that we have been justified, since justification puts an end to the legal strife between Judge and accused. Justification is a status or condition, a relationship which exists between God and those whom he justifies.

Let's remember Paul is preaching to the Jews in Rome, that right standing with God comes through faith rather than the law. With justification comes peace with God, for to be in right standing with God means there is no longer any animosity between God and the human race. Jesus' shed blood has brought us near to God.

Colossians 1:15–20
Christ is the visible image of the invisible God. He existed before anything was created and is supreme over all creation, for through him God created everything in the heavenly realms and on earth. He made the things we can see and the things we can't see such as thrones, kingdoms, rulers, and authorities in the unseen world. Everything was created through him and for him. He existed before anything else, and he holds all creation together. Christ is also the head of the church, which is his body. He is the beginning, supreme over all who rise from the dead. So he is first in everything. For God in all his fullness was pleased to live in Christ, and through him God reconciled everything to himself. He made peace with everything in

heaven and on earth by means of Christ's blood on the cross.

Ephesians 2:14–18
For Christ himself has brought peace to us. He united Jews and Gentiles into one people when, in his own body on the cross, he broke down the wall of hostility that separated us. He did this by ending the system of law with its commandments and regulations. He made peace between Jews and Gentiles by creating in himself one new people from the two groups. Together as one body, Christ reconciled both groups to God by means of his death on the cross, and our hostility toward each other was put to death. He brought this Good News of peace to you Gentiles who were far away from him, and peace to the Jews who were near. Now all of us can come to the Father through the same Holy Spirit because of what Christ has done for us.

Jesus has now joined Jews and Gentiles into one body, one group. Now we are the Church, members of His body. All people are the children of God. Together, Jew and Gentile are now a new people. No longer separated by race or culture, we are made new and placed in the family of God.

An Eternal Plan

Ephesians 3:6
And this is God's plan: Both Gentiles and Jews who believe the Good News share equally in the riches inherited by God's children. Both are part of the same body, and both enjoy the promise of blessings because they belong to Christ Jesus.

Ephesians 3:10–11
God's purpose in all this was to use the church to display his wisdom in its rich variety to all the unseen rulers and authorities in the heavenly places. This was his eternal plan, which he carried out through Christ Jesus our Lord.

God's purpose was to create one new people, which would become the Church. Through the church, God would reveal His wisdom to all the powers of the unseen world. All the demonic forces which were trying to destroy what God was doing would now be defeated by the faith of this new church. This was God's plan from the beginning. Paul calls it an eternal plan.

God knew before the entrance of sin in the Garden of Eden, that man would fall. He is Omniscient (All Knowing); God foreknew that his creation would sin, knowing this, God planned for this fall by sending his Son to die for his creation. We realize that Jesus did not come and die for man immediately following Adam's sin, but the Bible does tell us that Jesus planned to lay his life down for man before the world was created. Therefore, God's eternal plan would begin to unfold at the point of man's sin in the Garden of Eden.

1 Peter 1:18–20
For you know that God paid a ransom to save you from the empty life you inherited from your ancestors. And the ransom he paid was not mere gold or silver. It was the precious blood of Christ, the sinless, spotless Lamb of God. God chose him as your ransom long before the world began, but he has now revealed him to you in these last days.

Rejoicing in Troubles

Romans 5:3–5
We can rejoice, too, when we run into problems and trials, for we know that they help us develop endurance. And endurance develops strength of character, and character strengthens our confident hope of salvation. And this hope will not lead to disappointment. For we know how dearly God loves us, because he has given us the Holy Spirit to fill our hearts with his love.

Since believers can enjoy peace with God, how should they react to the trials of life? Now that we are no longer under the wrath of God we should rejoice in the trials and pressures life brings. We are free from God's anger which allows us to focus on how to live in this life with all its pressures.

Problems and trials is one Greek word meaning pressure, something which burdens us. Life is full of pressures, yet even in these we rejoice because we have peace with God and our eternity is secure.

2 Corinthians 4:16–18
That is why we never give up. Though our bodies are dying, our spirits are being renewed every day. For our present troubles are small and won't last very long. Yet they produce for us a glory that vastly outweighs them and will last forever! So we don't look at the troubles we can see now; rather, we fix our gaze on things that cannot be seen. For the things we see now will soon be gone, but the things we cannot see will last forever.

2 Corinthians 12:8–10
Three different times I begged the Lord to take it away. Each time he said, "My grace is all you need. My power works best in weakness." So now I am glad to boast about my weaknesses, so that the power of Christ can work through me. That's why I take pleasure in my weaknesses, and in the insults, hardships, persecutions, and troubles that I suffer for Christ. For when I am weak, then I am strong.

Suffering has its purpose just as the law had its purpose. Paul has just brought the Jewish people out of the law and into grace. The law was designed to reveal their sin and need for God's grace and peace. Now Paul contrasts the law with how the New Covenant works. No longer under punishment for failing to obey all the law we are under grace and free from God's wrath. BUT, in the natural there will be trouble, pressure and trials which are designed by God to help us grow and develop good character.

These pressures help us develop endurance which is patience; the ability to stand while under the pressure or the problem. We remain faithful to God even when under pressure.

Patience develops strength of character. Strength of character is the quality of being dependable and reliable. This dependability strengthens our expectation of the future of our salvation and the hope of eternal life promised us in Jesus Christ. This hope will never disappoint or bring to dishonor nor fail to fulfill God's purpose for this new people He has created.

All of this is guaranteed because we know how much God loves us and because we have been given the Holy Spirit, who has filled our hearts with His love. The Holy Spirit is the divine Agent who expresses to a believer the love of God, that is, God's love for him. The reality of God's love in a believer's heart gives the assurance, even the guarantee, that the believer's hope in God and His promise of glory is not misplaced and will not fail.

Christ came at the Right Time

Romans 5:6–7
When we were utterly helpless, Christ came at just the right time and died for us sinners. Now, most people would not be willing to die for an upright person, though someone might perhaps be willing to die for a person who is especially good.

Having mentioned the pouring out of God's love, Paul now described the character of God's love, which explains why its pouring out assures believers of hope. God demonstrated His love by the death of His Son, Jesus Christ. This demonstration was first, at just the right time. Second, it was when we were still powerless (without strength, feeble). Christ's death was a substitutionary death, a death in place of others or on behalf of others.

A person willing to die for another good person obviously is offering himself as a substitute so that the good person can continue to live. This is the highest expression of human love. However, God's love contrasts with human love in both nature and degree, because God demonstrates (keeps on showing) His own love for us in this: While we were still sinners, Christ died for us (in our place). Though a few people might possibly be willing to die to save the lives of good people, Christ went well beyond that. He died in the place of the powerless, the ungodly. The important point here is that God's love is better than human love. People could love someone they believe is good enough to be saved but, God s love will save even the ungodly and the unworthy.

God Reveals His Love through Jesus

Romans 5:8–11
But God showed his great love for us by sending Christ to die for us while we were still sinners. And since we have been made right in God's sight by the blood of Christ, he will certainly save us from God's condemnation. For since our friendship with God was restored by the death of his Son while we were still his enemies, we will certainly be saved through the life of his Son. So now we can rejoice in our wonderful new relationship with God because our Lord Jesus Christ has made us friends of God.

We have peace with God because He loves us! God proved His love for us by sending His Son to die for us while we were still unworthy and unholy. We have been made right with God by the blood of Jesus, not by our attempts of obedience to the law. We have been made right by faith in the blood of Jesus.

Now we can rejoice, despite the trials and pressures in our new relationship with God through Jesus Christ. This new way is so much superior to the law of the Old Testament in that the law could never make a person right with God. Now in Christ we are made right with God by believing in Jesus and the sacrifice He became.

This is in great contrast to what these believing Jews had been taught all their lives. Paul has taken them from feeling superior to all other peoples to being grateful for righteousness apart from the law, which they could never fully obey. Therefore, they were always subject to God's anger and punishment. Now through Jesus they are freed from their sin and made right with God without the need to physically submit to circumcision. Now through faith their hearts could be circumcised and the blood of Jesus would pay for their sin.

God revealed His love for us by sending Jesus to die for us. He did this while we were still in sin. This again is a new thought for these believing Jews. In the Mosaic covenant, they had to prove themselves first, then God would do something for them. Here Paul is revealing that God sent Jesus to die for them before they stopped sinning not afterwards. For them this is significant. In the Old system you sacrificed a lamb to cover you for the sins you had already committed. Now Jesus the lamb of God is covering their past as well as their future sins.

Romans 5:9–10
And since we have been made right in God's sight by the blood of Christ, he will certainly save us from God's condemnation. For since our friendship with God was restored by the death of his Son while we were still his

enemies, we will certainly be saved through the life of his Son.

The blood of Jesus is saving us from condemnation. Condemnation is the same word found in Chapter one translated as anger. It is better translated as wrath. The blood of Jesus has saved us from God's wrath.

We are not only saved from God's wrath but now our friendship with God has been restored. Friendship means to be reconciled with God. Our relationship with God is bought by the blood of Jesus. What Adam lost in the garden of Eden, Jesus restored with his blood.

Romans 5:11
So now we can rejoice in our wonderful new relationship with God because our Lord Jesus Christ has made us friends of God.

Rejoice is more often translated "glory or boast". an attitude of confidence in God. To rejoice in what Jesus has accomplished by his death and resurrection. We now experience peace with God through the wonderful work of Christ. We who were enemies of God have been brought near by the shed blood of the Son of God.

CHESTER GROSS

Chapter 9

How Sin Entered the World

Romans 5:12–15
When Adam sinned, sin entered the world. Adam's sin brought death, so death spread to everyone, for everyone sinned. Yes, people sinned even before the law was given. But it was not counted as sin because there was not yet any law to break. Still, everyone died—from the time of Adam to the time of Moses even those who did not disobey an explicit commandment of God, as Adam did. Now Adam is a symbol, a representation of Christ, who was yet to come. But there is a great difference between Adam's sin and God's gracious gift. For the sin of this one man, Adam, brought death to many. But even greater is

God's wonderful grace and his gift of forgiveness to many through this other man, Jesus Christ.

Paul had now finished his description of how God has revealed His righteousness based on the sacrificial death of Jesus Christ received by faith. One thing remains to be done, to present the difference between the work of Jesus Christ (and its results in justification and reconciliation) and the work of another man, Adam. Paul explained that sin entered the world through one man; and, in accord with God's warning, death through sin. God's penalty for sin was both spiritual and physical death, and Adam and Eve and their descendants experienced both. Paul concluded, and in this way death came to all men. "Came" is literally "passed or went through" or "spread through." "entered into" which means that sin went in the world's front door (by means of Adam's sin); and "went through," means that death penetrated the entire human race, like a vapor permeating all a house's rooms. The reason death spread to all, Paul explained, is that all sinned.

All men were made sinners through Adams sin. We are not condemned to hell because we sin but because of the sin nature given to all men through Adam. When Adam disobeyed, he caused all men to be born with a sinful nature, this nature is then passed to all men even though they did not commit the same sin as Adam. All people go to hell because they reject Jesus Christ and have a sin nature. All who accept Christ receive a new nature and are born again. This is what gives them the right to go to heaven. This seems to be hard for people to understand because we are so aware of our sin. First John tells us that if anyone says they have no sin they are liars and do not have God. So, the truth is that every Christian sins but, the nature of sin is broken in Christ.

Romans 5:14
Still, everyone died from the time of Adam to the time of Moses even those who did not disobey an explicit commandment of God, as Adam did. Now Adam is a symbol, a representation of Christ, who was yet to come.

Circumcision was the covenantal sign of the Mosaic covenant. This circumcision was the physical removal of a piece of skin from a man's body where life originates and where his gender is identified. This skin never grows back. In the new covenant, God circumcised our hearts and cut away the old Adamic sin nature and removed it from us.

The Bible makes it very clear that sin entered into the human race through one man, by the fall of Adam. Adam was created with no disposition towards evil; yet Adam himself commits a sin. God didn't cause the fall of Adam, but once Adam chose to sin, God's punishment was to allow Adam to deteriorate into a fallen moral condition, which moral condition is then transmitted to all future descendants.

Original sin refers to the result of the first sin, not the first sin itself. Original sin is not a specific sin, an act of disobedience; it must do with the nature of mankind. The Bible tells us that our nature is fallen, that not only do we sin, but we are pervaded by sin, that is, our natures are corrupt. Jesus put it this way: a bad tree brings forth corrupt fruit. It is not that we are sinful because we sin, but rather that we sin because we are sinful. The activity of sin flows out of a sinful nature, a fallen nature, a heart that is out of sync with God. Man, is fallen in the depths of his being, and he has a basic disposition towards sin rather than towards righteousness.

Therefore, just stopping sin does not change the heart. This was the problem of the law. It could not change the nature within people, therefore, sin remained. Adam's sin made all people sinners by nature, now in Christ we are given a new nature. A changed heart, a new nature we are now a new creation in Christ Jesus and have been set free from the sin of Adam.

Most Christians do not understand the grace of God. Grace saves us without the need to be holy. Yet, grace will cause a person to be holy because it is based on the new nature. Once we accept Christ we become a new creature. This new man has new desires; he longs to please God and begins seeking to be holy like God is holy. I still have not met a Christian that wakes up every morning with a desire to walk in a lifestyle of sin.

The law could never defeat sin, but grace always defeats sin. If the law could bring holiness to men, then Christ would not have had to come. Jesus came because the law could not produce righteousness, therefore He came and died to redeem us from the law and free us from the sin nature caused by Adam's sin. All men are sinners through Adam's sin and all men are made righteous through the death of Christ.

Romans 5:15–16
But there is a great difference between Adam's sin and God's gracious gift. For the sin of this one man, Adam, brought death to many. But even greater is God's wonderful grace and his gift of forgiveness to many through this other man, Jesus Christ. And the result of God's gracious gift is very different from the result of that one man's sin. For Adam's sin led to condemnation, but God's free gift leads to our being made right with God, even though we are guilty of many sins.

Paul brings the contrast between the sin of Adam and the gift from Jesus Christ. The work of Jesus Christ is far greater in releasing God's grace freely to all mankind than the sin of Adam in causing all people to become sinners.

The gift of God leads to our being right with God even though we were guilty of many sins. It is the one sin of Adam which brought sin to all mankind. We all commit many sins, this is not Paul's concern. He is speaking to the one sin committed by Adam which Jesus redeems us from.

Romans 5:17
For the sin of this one man, Adam, caused death to rule over many. But even greater is God's wonderful grace and his gift of righteousness, for all who receive it will live in triumph over sin and death through this one man, Jesus Christ.

Paul is saying that the power and impact of the Second Adam is much greater than the impact of the first Adam. The impact of Adam has been awful, it has put men in misery, in ruin. But the solution is infinitely greater, because Christ has abounded in winning eternal life for men.

Romans 5:18–19
Yes, Adam's one sin brings condemnation for everyone, but Christ's one act of righteousness brings a right relationship with God and new life for everyone. Because one person disobeyed God, many became sinners. But because one other person obeyed God, many will be made righteous.

Jesus's act of obedience that reverses Adam's disobedience, alludes back to his death for us in the Father's loving design. Paul elsewhere defines Jesus's obedience in terms of humbling himself to the point of shameful execution on a cross, perhaps in contrast to

Adam seeking divinity. Adam, by seeking greater life, brought death, whereas Jesus by dying brought life. Just as Adam introduced sin, Jesus now introduces true righteousness that stems from solidarity with his obedience. Paul's understanding is not that Jesus merely reverses Adam's punishment, but that Jesus came to form a new basis for humanity, enabling people to serve God fully from the heart.

Return to the Law

Romans 5:20–21
God's law was given so that all people could see how sinful they were. But as people sinned more and more, God's wonderful grace became more abundant. So just as sin ruled over all people and brought them to death, now God's wonderful grace rules instead, giving us right standing with God and resulting in eternal life through Jesus Christ our Lord.

Again, the law was a teacher put in charge to lead us to Christ. Now that faith has come we no longer are to live under the law. This is one of the areas the church has missed. The church is still trying to mix both covenants.

Galatians 3:19-29
What, then, was the purpose of the law? It was added because of transgressions until the Seed to whom the promise referred had come. The law was put into effect

through angels by a mediator. A mediator, however, does not represent just one party; but God is one. Is the law, therefore, opposed to the promises of God? Absolutely not! For if a law had been given that could impart life, then righteousness would certainly have come by the law. But the Scripture declares that the whole world is a prisoner of sin, so that what was promised, being given through faith in Jesus Christ, might be given to those who believe. Before this faith came, we were held prisoners by the law, locked up until faith should be revealed. So the law was put in charge to lead us to Christ that we might be justified by faith. Now that faith has come, we are no longer under the supervision of the law. You are all sons of God through faith in Christ Jesus, for all of you who were baptized into Christ have clothed yourselves with Christ. There is neither Jew nor Greek, slave nor free, male nor female, for you are all one in Christ Jesus. If you belong to Christ, then you are Abraham's seed, and heirs according to the promise.

Before faith came men were kept guarded, kept in captivity, held prisoner. The thought of this verse is well stated in the NIV: "Before this faith came, we were held prisoners by the law, locked up until faith should be revealed."

The law was our schoolmaster, a child-conductor. The Greeks gave a faithful servant the responsibility of taking care of a boy from childhood to puberty. The servant kept him from both physical and moral evil, and went with him during play and school, but he did not teach him.

Until Christ could come as the object of faith, the law had to act as a child-custodian for us. The law acted as an outward check on desires, making the consciousness of sin more acute. It further emphasized that man is unable to deal with sin, guiding him to Christ. The moral law shows what man ought to do, and he learns his inability to do it.

Paul sums up this chapter by saying that God's grace rules instead of the law and grace now brings right standing with God which results in eternal life.

Chapter 10

Shall we continue to Sin?

Romans 6:1–4
Well then, should we keep on sinning so that God can show us more and more of his wonderful grace? Of course not! Since we have died to sin, how can we continue to live in it? Or have you forgotten that when we were joined with Christ Jesus in baptism, we joined him in his death? For we died and were buried with Christ by baptism. And just as Christ was raised from the dead by the glorious power of the Father, now we also may live new lives.

At the close of chapter five, Paul seems to be saying that whenever men sin, God moves in with grace, and the more sin there is, the more grace there is. An evil person could jump on that statement and distort it as a licence to sin. He may say, 'If sin is an occasion for God to give a greater portion of grace, then the more I sin, the more God is going to send grace into the world to counteract it. Therefore, I am called of God to add to the sin in the world!'

Paul anticipates that kind of distortion at the beginning of chapter six: What shall we say, then? Shall we go on sinning, so that grace may increase? How does he answer it? By no means! We died to sin; how can we live in it any longer? Such an idea is utterly unthinkable for anybody with a Christian heart and a Christian mind.

Paul will make the point in this chapter that since we have joined Christ in baptism we have also been buried with him. We have been given a new nature. This new nature changes the natural inclination to sin. Since our nature has changed, why would anyone want to continue in sin? It doesn't make sense to Paul.

Paul asks the question, "have we forgotten that when we were joined with Jesus in baptism we died with him? Since we have been buried with Christ we are also raised to a new life. This new life should prevent us from continuing in sin.

Galatians 3:26–27
For you are all children of God through faith in Christ Jesus. And all who have been united with Christ in baptism have put on Christ, like putting on new clothes.

1 Peter 3:21
And that water is a picture of baptism, which now saves you, not by removing dirt from your body, but as a response to God from a clean conscience. It is effective because of the resurrection of Jesus Christ.

Baptism cleanses our conscience from sin. Through baptism we are united with Christ. This happens because we have received a new nature through faith in the work of Christ. We become a new person.

2 Corinthians 5:17
This means that anyone who belongs to Christ has become a new person. The old life is gone; a new life has begun!

We have been Crucified with Christ

Romans 6:5–11
Since we have been united with him in his death, we will also be raised to life as he was. We know that our old sinful selves were crucified with Christ so that sin might lose its power in our lives. We are no longer slaves to sin. For when we died with Christ we were set free from the power of sin. And since we died with Christ, we know we

will also live with him. We are sure of this because Christ was raised from the dead, and he will never die again. Death no longer has any power over him. When he died, he died once to break the power of sin. But now that he lives, he lives for the glory of God. So you also should consider yourselves to be dead to the power of sin and alive to God through Christ Jesus.

When he says that we are dead to sin, does this mean that we don't sin at all? Of course not. He makes it clear in chapter seven that the Christian is not free from the battle with sin. But the death sentence has been pronounced upon the old nature. I have been crucified with Jesus Christ, representatively. In God's sight my evil nature is dead. My sin was put to death on the cross of Jesus Christ and my sins were paid for. I was released from the bondage to sin.

Jesus Broke the Power of Sin

Romans 6:9–11
We are sure of this because Christ was raised from the dead, and he will never die again. Death no longer has any power over him. When he died, he died once to break the power of sin. But now that he lives, he lives for the glory of God. So you also should consider yourselves to be dead to the power of sin and alive to God through Christ Jesus.

Jesus was raised from the dead and can never die

again. When he died, He broke the power and dominion of sin. Since Jesus has conquered sin we should consider ourselves dead to the controlling power of sin. We are no longer bound by sin through the sin nature. Now we are set free from the nature of sin which forces us into sin. With a new nature, we now have a choice.

Romans 6:12–13
Do not let sin control the way you live; do not give in to sinful desires. Do not let any part of your body become an instrument of evil to serve sin. Instead, give yourselves completely to God, for you were dead, but now you have new life. So use your whole body as an instrument to do what is right for the glory of God.

Now that we have a choice to stop sinning we are to control the way we live and abstain from the desires which lead us into sin. Now we are to use our bodies to do what is right before God.

Galatians 5:16-17
So I say, live by the Spirit, and you will not gratify the desires of the sinful nature. For the sinful nature desires what is contrary to the Spirit, and the Spirit what is contrary to the sinful nature. They are in conflict with each other, so that you do not do what you want. But if you are led by the Spirit, you are not under law.

Once we have been born again we are given a new

nature. Our spirit man, before Christ was dead. The term "dead" means to be inactive. When we were sinners by nature our spirit was considered dead to God. That is why the term "born again" is used to describe someone who has been made alive in Christ. Our human spirit is regenerated or made new by the Holy Spirit when we accept Christ. This act of regeneration is what gives us a new nature. When we accept Christ, the Holy Spirit comes and quickens our spirit and then indwells our spirit and we become His temple. Once we have become regenerated in our spirit our desires begin to change. We no longer want the same things as before. We now have a hunger for God and the Word of God. We now desire holiness and purity.

Galatians 5:24-25
Those who belong to Christ Jesus have crucified the sinful nature with its passions and desires. Since we live by the Spirit, let us keep in step with the Spirit.

We have now put off the sinful nature. Before, we followed the world and its system and gratified the desires of our sinful nature but now, in Christ, we have been made alive and saved by grace. When we accepted Christ, we put off the old person and his nature and we became a new person who has a new nature.

Ephesians 2:1-5
As for you, you were dead in your transgressions and sins, in which you used to live when you followed the ways of

this world and of the ruler of the kingdom of the air, the spirit who is now at work in those who are disobedient. All of us also lived among them at one time, gratifying the cravings of our sinful nature and following its desires and thoughts. Like the rest, we were by nature objects of wrath. But because of his great love for us, God, who is rich in mercy, made us alive with Christ even when we were dead in transgressions - it is by grace you have been saved.

Colossians 2:9-14
For in Christ all the fullness of the Deity lives in bodily form, and you have been given fullness in Christ, who is the head over every power and authority. In him you were also circumcised, in the putting off of the sinful nature, not with a circumcision done by the hands of men but with the circumcision done by Christ, having been buried with him in baptism and raised with him through your faith in the power of God, who raised him from the dead. When you were dead in your sins and in the un-circumcision of your sinful nature, God made you alive with Christ. He forgave us all our sins, having canceled the written code, with its regulations, that was against us and that stood opposed to us; he took it away, nailing it to the cross.

Colossians 3:9-10
Do not lie to each other, since you have taken off your old self with its practices and have put on the new self, which is being renewed in knowledge in the image of its Creator.

Jesus redeemed us from sin through his blood and brought to us the forgiveness of God. He abundantly gave us God's grace and revealed to us the mystery of his will. His will was that we would be saved from the wrath of God due to our sin.

Ephesians 1:7-14
In him we have redemption through his blood, the forgiveness of sins, in accordance with the riches of God's grace that he lavished on us with all wisdom and understanding. And he made known to us the mystery of his will according to his good pleasure, which he purposed in Christ, to be put into effect when the times will have reached their fulfillment to bring all things in heaven and on earth together under one head, even Christ. In him we were also chosen, having been predestined according to the plan of him who works out everything in conformity with the purpose of his will, in order that we, who were the first to hope in Christ, might be for the praise of his glory. And you also were included in Christ when you heard the word of truth, the gospel of your salvation. Having believed, you were marked in him with a seal, the promised Holy Spirit, who is a deposit guaranteeing our inheritance until the redemption of those who are God's possession to the praise of his glory.

Grace has been poured out on us through the redemption given us through the shed blood of Jesus Christ. Forgiveness of our sins is now a reality.

Sin is no longer your Master

Romans 6:14
Sin is no longer your master, for you no longer live under the requirements of the law. Instead, you live under the freedom of God's grace.

Here Paul brings in the contrast of the law and grace. One important thing to notice is that if we live under the law we are still under the power of sin. Once the power of sin is broken, obedience to the law is no longer required.

Galatians 2:19
For through the law I died to the law so that I might live for God.

Romans 8:1-2
Therefore, there is now no condemnation for those who are in Christ Jesus, because through Christ Jesus the law of the Spirit of life set me free from the law of sin and death.

Galatians 3:23-25
Before this faith came, we were held prisoners by the law, locked up until faith should be revealed. So the law was put in charge to lead us to Christ that we might be justified by faith. Now that faith has come, we are no longer under the supervision

These scriptures clearly reveal the purpose of the law

and its end. First, we are dead to the law so we can now live for God. Second, the Holy Spirit has set us free from the law which causes sin and results in death. Finally, the law held us in prison to sin until Christ would come. Now that faith has come we are no longer under the law.

Paul clearly explains the issue with the law and the importance of faith. Now we move into grace, Paul again askes the question "shall we continue to sin because we are under grace?" This is the second time in this chapter Paul asks the same question.

Romans 6:15–16
Well then, since God's grace has set us free from the law, does that mean we can go on sinning? Of course not! Don't you realize that you become the slave of whatever you choose to obey? You can be a slave to sin, which leads to death, or you can choose to obey God, which leads to righteous living.

Paul asks the question a second time. "Since God's grace has set us free form the law does that mean we can go on sinning?" Of course not! We have a choice, we can obey sin or God, each carries consequence.

God's design is that sin shall not be your master "shall not rule as lord". The reason sin should not master you is because you are not under Law, but under grace. Paul had already explained that "the Law was added so that the trespass might increase" (5:20), and elsewhere he declared, "The power of sin is the Law" (1 Cor. 15:56). If believers were still under the Law, it would be impossible to keep sin from exercising mastery. But since believers are "under grace," mastery over sin can be accomplished by following Paul's instructions.

Paul again shocks the sensibilities of his audience by reversing traditional expectations. It is those under the law rather than those under grace who are prone to sin (6:14–15), which he will soon identify with lawlessness (6:19).

Slaves to what we Choose to Obey

Romans 6:16
Don't you realize that you become the slave of whatever you choose to obey? You can be a slave to sin, which leads to death, or you can choose to obey God, which leads to righteous living.

Freedom from the Law does not give one license to sin. Christians have simply exchanged masters; they have not expelled morality. Christians now have a choice to serve their new master in righteousness or return to the old taskmaster of sin and experience death.

Romans 6:17–18
Thank God! Once you were slaves of sin, but now you wholeheartedly obey this teaching we have given you.

Now you are free from your slavery to sin, and you have become slaves to righteous living.

Prior to becoming Christians, the readers were in bondage to sin. However, this is not their present position. Paul wants to convey that deliverance from sin's mastery begins by faith in Christ (through dying with Him in Spirit baptism), and continues by obedience to this faith. To confirm the new status and realm where believers reside, Paul uses "freedom" language for the first time, saying that we have been set free from sin. Because of being set free, all believers are now legal slaves of God, and therefore free to resist sin and live as slaves of righteousness.

Sinful Nature

Romans 6:19
Because of the weakness of your human nature, I am using the illustration of slavery to help you understand all this. Previously, you let yourselves be slaves to impurity and lawlessness, which led ever deeper into sin. Now you must give yourselves to be slaves to righteous living so that you will become holy.

The weakness of the sin nature caused us to be slaves to the nature of sin which led us deeper and deeper into sin. Now we have a choice. We must now give ourselves to serve the new nature and live righteously so that we will become holy.

Unsaved Romans had offered their bodies to impurity and to ever-increasing lawlessness. They had voluntarily become enslaved! But Paul exhorted believers now to offer themselves as slaves to righteousness leading to holiness which is the end of the sanctification process in contrast to their former impurity.

Romans 6:20–22
When you were slaves to sin, you were free from the obligation to do right. And what was the result? You are now ashamed of the things you used to do, things that end in eternal doom. But now you are free from the power of sin and have become slaves of God. Now you do those things that lead to holiness and result in eternal life.

Sanctification is the result of this new, and willing, slavery to God. Holiness is being increasingly conformed to the image of God in Christ. Putting off the old, being adorned with the new. These concepts, these realities, should be the delight and goal of each believer. Nothing should suppress the longing for personal holiness that the Spirit has implanted in our hearts.

We can now become holy (sanctified) because we have a new nature. No longer are we slaves to the sin nature, we are free to do the things which lead to holiness and result in eternal life. We have a choice! Under the law there was not a choice. We were born in sin and in sin we stayed. The law only revealed sin it could not remove it.

Now, through a new nature, we are free from the law which causes sin to increase. God's incredible grace has come through faith in Jesus Christ and we have been given the gift of righteousness.

Romans 6:23
For the wages of sin is death, but the free gift of God is eternal life through Christ Jesus our Lord.

Servants of sin earn wages; they get what they deserve. But eternal life in Jesus Christ our Lord is a gift from God. A gift cannot be purchased. A gift cannot be earned. A gift cannot be merited. It is something that God gives freely.

Chapter 11

Conflicting Natures

In chapter five Paul discusses the cause of mankind's fall and the redemption of the human race. Adam's sin brought sin and death to all people even to those who did not commit the same sin as Adam. Jesus brought righteousness to all people through his death and resurrection.

Chapter six focuses on the contrast of these two natures, one which leads to death and the other to peace with God. Now that the sin nature is put to death through faith in Christ and identification with baptism we have a choice. We can follow the practices of the sin nature or, through the new nature we can do what is right before God.

The choice is ours for the first time in the history of the world. Adam's sin caused the power of the sin nature to rule over the human race. Now through Jesus the power of the sin nature is defeated. With a new nature, we are freed from the control of the sin nature so we can now choose whom we will serve. Therefore, Paul states, don't give the members of your body to acts of unrighteousness.

Now in chapter seven Paul goes back to the law which was strengthened by the sin nature. He opens chapter seven with an example of the law.

Romans 7:1–3
Now, dear brothers and sisters you who are familiar with the law don't you know that the law applies only while a person is living? For example, when a woman marries, the law binds her to her husband if he is alive. But if he dies, the laws of marriage no longer apply to her. So while her husband is alive, she would be committing adultery if she married another man. But if her husband dies, she is free from that law and does not commit adultery when she remarries.

Divorce

Paul begins with an example of what the law says. Paul is not communicating a doctrine on divorce it is merely an illustration. He begins, "you who are familiar with the law, you know what the law says."

For example, when a woman marries she is bound to her husband until he dies then she is no longer under the rules of marriage. Paul is again building a case against the need for the law to govern our lives. Faith has given us a new nature which replaces the need for the law to govern us.

Romans 7:4–6
So, my dear brothers and sisters, this is the point: You died to the power of the law when you died with Christ. And now you are united with the one who was raised from the dead. As a result, we can produce a harvest of good deeds for God. When we were controlled by our old nature, sinful desires were at work within us, and the law aroused these evil desires that produced a harvest of sinful deeds, resulting in death. But now we have been released from the law, for we died to it and are no longer captive to its power. Now we can serve God, not in the old way of obeying the letter of the law, but in the new way of living in the Spirit.

Here is the Point

We died to the law through the death of Christ, now

we are united with Jesus. The result is that now we CAN do what is right before God. Now we can serve God in a new way in the Spirit rather than the old way. We are no longer controlled by the sin nature. Therefore, we are freed from the control of the law. The law aroused the desires of the sin nature, which produced sinful behavior.

Remember the illustration of divorce? The point is: just as a wife is free from the rules of marriage if her husband dies so we are free from the law because we died to the sin nature.

Romans 7:4 NIV
So, my brothers, you also died to the law through the body of Christ, that you might belong to another, to him who was raised from the dead, in order that we might bear fruit to God.

We died to the power of the law so that you might belong to another. The point is we cannot belong to Christ if we are still married to the law through the sin nature. We must die to the sin nature to be united with Christ. Paul used the example of marriage and divorce to illustrate the need for our death to the sin nature to allow us to become married to Christ.

A New Way of the Spirit

The new nature is the way of the Spirit. The new

nature is controlled by the Holy Spirit. Through faith we enter a new covenant with God in which the Holy Spirit puts to death the sin nature in us and replaces it with a new nature called righteousness. This new nature creates a new way controlled and led by the Holy Spirit's influence. Now we are led by the Holy Spirit and no longer need the law.

Galatians 5:16–18
So I say, let the Holy Spirit guide your lives. Then you won't be doing what your sinful nature craves. The sinful nature wants to do evil, which is just the opposite of what the Spirit wants. And the Spirit gives us desires that are the opposite of what the sinful nature desires. These two forces are constantly fighting each other, so you are not free to carry out your good intentions. But when you are directed by the Spirit, you are not under obligation to the law of Moses.

Galatians 3:1–3
Oh, foolish Galatians! Who has cast an evil spell on you? For the meaning of Jesus Christ's death was made as clear to you as if you had seen a picture of his death on the cross. Let me ask you this one question: Did you receive the Holy Spirit by obeying the law of Moses? Of course not! You received the Spirit because you believed the message you heard about Christ. How foolish can you be? After starting your new lives in the Spirit, why are you now trying to become perfect by your own human effort?

The Roman Christians are so obsessed with the law that they just can't let it go. Paul masterfully states his case that the law cannot produce righteousness in people. Therefore, to go back to the law was to reject the Spirit and go back to human effort to gain right standing with God.

Struggle with Sin

Romans 7:7–8
Well then, am I suggesting that the law of God is sinful? Of course, not! In fact, it was the law that showed me my sin. I would never have known that coveting is wrong if the law had not said, "You must not covet." But sin used this command to arouse all kinds of covetous desires within me! If there were no law, sin would not have that power.

Paul continually uses this argument about the law. Is the law bad, is it sin? Of course not! The law shows us our sin. Therefore, once sin is revealed it arouses the desire for the sin it sees. Without a new nature, the desire once revealed defeats the ability to resist and sin is in control.

Romans 7:9–12
At one time I lived without understanding the law. But when I learned the command not to covet, for instance, the power of sin came to life, and I died. So I discovered that the law's commands, which were supposed to bring life, brought spiritual death instead. Sin took advantage of

those commands and deceived me; it used the commands to kill me. But still, the law itself is holy, and its commands are holy and right and good.

The sin nature took advantage of the law to produce sin in us. The law still was good, holy and right, yet, it could not defeat the sin nature given to us through Adam. Only a new nature through Jesus could make us right with God and defeat the control of sin in us.

Romans 7:13
But how can that be? Did the law, which is good, cause my death? Of course not! Sin used what was good to bring about my condemnation to death. So we can see how terrible sin really is. It uses God's good commands for its own evil purposes.

How can this be? The sin nature used God's law for its own evil purpose. The law relied on our own human efforts to obey. The sin nature used our weakness to exploit the law through our own desires.

James 1:13–15
And remember, when you are being tempted, do not say, "God is tempting me." God is never tempted to do wrong, and he never tempts anyone else. Temptation comes from our own desires, which entice us and drag us away. These desires give birth to sinful actions. And when sin is allowed to grow, it gives birth to death.

The problem was not the law it was our desires which were controlled by a sinful nature. We were doomed from the start. Is it any surprise that Paul says the new covenant is founded with better promises? Thank God for Jesus Christ and his death and resurrection putting to death the sin nature. Without Christ, we would still be in our sin and under the control of sin.

The Conflict

Romans 7:14–17
So the trouble is not with the law, for it is spiritual and good. The trouble is with me, for I am all too human, a slave to sin. I don't really understand myself, for I want to do what is right, but I don't do it. Instead, I do what I hate. But if I know that what I am doing is wrong, this shows that I agree that the law is good. So I am not the one doing wrong; it is sin living in me that does it.

The problem is not the law it is US! Before we are in Christ the sin nature makes us slaves to sin, which makes us unable to do what is right. When we want to do right we still do wrong. Notice, it is not me doing it but the sin nature which is in me. This is referring to a person who still have a sin nature.

Romans 7:18–20
And I know that nothing good lives in me, that is, in my sinful nature. I want to do what is right, but I can't. I want

to do what is good, but I don't. I don't want to do what is wrong, but I do it anyway. But if I do what I don't want to do, I am not really the one doing wrong; it is sin living in me that does it.

Notice the context here! We are talking about the sin nature in us. Here is where most people see the duality of both natures still living in us. This is not what Paul is saying. Notice the next verses.

Romans 7:21–24
I have discovered this principle of life that when I want to do what is right, I inevitably do what is wrong. I love God's law with all my heart. But there is another power within me that is at war with my mind. This power makes me a slave to the sin that is still within me. Oh, what a miserable person I am! Who will free me from this life that is dominated by sin and death?

The principle is that if the sin nature lives in me I will continue to do wrong even though I love God and want to obey the law I will still sin. There is a battle that exists in people with a sin nature which creates a war within their mind. They want to do good but are unable to do it. The sin nature has control of them producing death.

The Body

The battle is in our minds which control our physical

bodies. In chapter six, Paul, encourages us not to let any part of our body become an instrument of evil. Rather, to give our body to God.

Romans 6:13–14
Do not let any part of your **body** become an instrument of evil to serve sin. Instead, give yourselves completely to God, for you were dead, but now you have new life. So use your whole **body** as an instrument to do what is right for the glory of God. Sin is no longer your master, for you no longer live under the requirements of the law. Instead, you live under the freedom of God's grace.

Romans 8:13 NIV
For if you live according to the sinful nature, you will die; but if by the Spirit you put to death the misdeeds of the body, you will live.

Paul is talking about the problem which exists with our physical bodies. We must put to death the misdeeds of the body. We could not accomplish this if we do not have a new nature. The power and control of sin is broken through a new nature. Now the body must submit to God to become holy.

Romans 7:23 NIV
But I see another law at work in the members of my **body**, waging war against the law of my mind and making me a prisoner of the law of sin at work within my members.

In chapter twelve we are commanded to present our bodies as a living sacrifice, holy and pleasing to God. This is done through the renewal of our minds. Notice, that the war is between the body and the mind.

Romans 12:1–2 NIV
Therefore, I urge you, brothers, in view of God's mercy, to offer your bodies as living sacrifices, holy and pleasing to God this is your spiritual act of worship. Do not conform any longer to the pattern of this world, but be transformed by the renewing of your mind. Then you will be able to test and approve what God's will is his good, pleasing and perfect will.

Even though we have a new nature we still have an unrenewed mind and a body not yet glorified. These two aspects are still in process. Sanctification is the process of transforming the mind, will and emotions to the Holy Spirit and creates holiness. Glorification is the final work of salvation, bringing immortality and purity to the physical body.

This is so clear. We do not have a dual nature, Paul is talking about those who still have a sin nature not those with a new nature. The confusion of these verses comes because Paul has been using third person language, then in this section he changes to first person. Then in chapter eight Paul goes back to third person. In chapter seven verse six Paul says, "now WE can serve God in the new way of the Spirit." Then in verse seven he switches to I and me. This language causes us to think Paul is talking about himself in the present. Paul began chapter seven with an illustration of the law then says in verse five, "When we were controlled by our old nature, sinful desires were at work within us, and the law aroused these evil desires that produced a harvest of sinful deeds, resulting in death."

Paul uses the past tense "when" referring to the old nature. Then a few verses later he talks about the problem he faces with this old nature, making us think he is talking in the present tense. I believe Paul is still giving an example of his own life. When he had an old nature, these were the problems he faced, BUT NOW he is freed from the old sin nature. Next look at Romans 8:7-9, where Paul again asserts that we are not controlled by the sin nature if the Spirit of God lives in us. We cannot justify a dual nature if all verses before chapter seven verse seven and all verses after this section say we no longer have a new nature. We must stay in context.

The battle is not between two natures but rather, between an unrenewed mind and a body not yet free from corruption and decay. Paul, discusses the issue of corruption and decay in the chapter eight.

Sin Nature

Romans 8:7–9
For the sinful nature is always hostile to God. It never did obey God's laws, and it never will. That's why those who are still under the control of their sinful nature can never please God. But **you are not controlled by your sinful nature. You are controlled by the Spirit if you have the Spirit of God living in you.** (And remember that those who do not have the Spirit of Christ living in them do not belong to him at all.)

The sin nature is always hostile to God. It cannot ever obey God. You are NOT controlled by the sinful nature IF the Spirit of God lives in you. Our spirits are regenerated by the Holy Spirit. Regeneration is the process which renews our spirit and gives us a new nature. If regeneration has taken place we know we have a new nature.

Colossians 3:9–10
Don't lie to each other, for you have stripped off your old sinful nature and all its wicked deeds. Put on your new nature, and be renewed as you learn to know your Creator and become like him.

Romans 7:5–6
When we were controlled by our old nature, sinful desires were at work within us, and the law aroused these evil desires that produced a harvest of sinful deeds, resulting in death. **But now we have been released from**

the law, for we died to it and are no longer captive to its power. Now we can serve God, not in the old way of obeying the letter of the law, but in the new way of living in the Spirit.

1 Timothy 1:9–11
For the law was not intended for people who do what is right. It is for people who are lawless and rebellious, who are ungodly and sinful, who consider nothing sacred and defile what is holy, who kill their father or mother or commit other murders. The law is for people who are sexually immoral, or who practice homosexuality, or are slave traders, liars, promise breakers, or who do anything else that contradicts the wholesome teaching that comes from the glorious Good News entrusted to me by our blessed God.

It is clear! Two natures cannot exist in you at the same time. We have died to the sin nature, we are free. The sin nature cannot please God, who can deliver us from this problem? Only Jesus Christ! Paul states that we no longer have a sin nature. In Timothy, Paul tells us who the law was for. Remember the law was to govern the sin nature not the new nature.

Do we as followers of Jesus reflect this list? This is clearly talking about those with a sinful nature. Followers of Jesus are capable of obeying God. Timothy says these people are ungodly and consider nothing to be sacred. This is not a follower of Jesus with a new nature.

Finally, Paul gives us the answer to the dilemma of doing wrong when we want to do right. The answer as we will see in chapter eight is a new nature.

Romans 7:25
Thank God! The answer is in Jesus Christ our Lord. So you see how it is: In my mind I really want to obey God's law, but because of my sinful nature I am a slave to sin.

Jesus Christ is the answer to the sin nature. He breaks the power of sin and releases us from sins control, then places a new nature in us. Now we can obey God because the Spirit of God lives in us and he helps us with our weaknesses and produces holiness in us.

Chapter eight further explores this issue. Paul declares in the first two verses the answer to this problem.

Romans 8:1–2
So now there is no condemnation for those who belong to Christ Jesus. And because you belong to him, the power of the life-giving Spirit has freed you from the power of sin that leads to death.

Chapter 12

No Condemnation

Chapter seven ends with the question, "who will free me from this life of sin and death?" Thank God! The answer is Jesus Christ our Lord. Paul ends chapter seven here and begins chapter eight with, "there is no longer any condemnation."

Romans 8:1–2
So now there is no condemnation for those who belong to Christ Jesus. And because you belong to him, the power of the life-giving Spirit has freed you from the power of sin that leads to death.

Paul contrasts two principles, what he calls two laws. On the one hand, there is the law of the Spirit of life in Christ Jesus, and on the other hand, there is the law of sin and death.

When we had a sinful nature, we were exposed to the penalties of the law which included eternal death. We were controlled by the sin nature. Now another law has been revealed, the law of the Spirit of life in Christ Jesus, which is a new nature. Paul is showing the power of the gospel to set us free from the control of the sin nature.

Condemnation is the legal decision of guilty in a criminal case, often with the punishment already understood. Adam's sin brought us a guilty verdict with the penalty of eternal death.

Romans 5:18–19
Yes, Adam's one sin brings condemnation for everyone, but Christ's one act of righteousness brings a right relationship with God and new life for everyone. Because one person disobeyed God, many became sinners. But because one other person obeyed God, many will be made righteous.

This new law, the Spirit of life, frees us from the law of sin and releases us from the punishment of eternal death. The law was unable to save us because of the sinful nature. Now in Jesus we receive a new nature when we believe. This new nature frees us from the sin nature and its impending punishment.

Romans 8:3–4
The law of Moses was unable to save us because of the weakness of our sinful nature. So God did what the law could not do. He sent his own Son in a body like the bodies we sinners have. And in that body God declared an end to sin's control over us by giving his Son as a sacrifice for our sins. He did this so that the just requirement of the law would be fully satisfied for us, who no longer follow our sinful nature but instead follow the Spirit.

Jesus did what the law was unable to do. His death brought an end to the sin nature for all those who believe. Jesus became a man that he might fulfil the requirements of the law and pay the penalty we deserved with his blood. The sacrifice of Jesus broke sin's control over us.

Galatians 4:4–7
But when the right time came, God sent his Son, born of a woman, subject to the law. God sent him to buy freedom for us who were slaves to the law, so that he could adopt us as his very own children. And because we are his children, God has sent the Spirit of his Son into our hearts, prompting us to call out, "Abba, Father." Now you are no longer a slave but God's own child. And since you are his child, God has made you his heir.

We have been adopted by God. Now, we are no longer slaves to the sin nature but are the children of God and heirs with Jesus Christ. We receive a new nature through the Holy Spirit imparted in our human spirit by faith in Jesus. This faith now saves us and releases us from the law of sin and death.

Sin Nature cannot Please God

Romans 8:5–8
Those who are dominated by the sinful nature think about sinful things, but those who are controlled by the Holy Spirit think about things that please the Spirit. So letting your sinful nature control your mind leads to death. But letting the Spirit control your mind leads to life and peace. For the sinful nature is always hostile to God. It never did obey God's laws, and it never will. That's why those who are still under the control of their sinful nature can never please God.

Paul continues this contrast between the Spirit (new nature) and the sinful nature: Those who live according to the sinful nature always think about what the nature desires; but those who are controlled by the Spirit think about what will please the Spirit. When we receive the new nature, the Holy Spirit lives in us. We become His temple.

Once our nature is changed our desires change. We

are no longer controlled by the sin nature which controls our thoughts and leads us to sinful acts. Now, we think about how we can please God. That is why those who are controlled by the sin nature can never please God. They are hostile towards God and cannot obey Him at all.

Galatians 5:16
So I say, let the Holy Spirit guide your lives. Then you won't be doing what your sinful nature craves.

We are not Controlled by the Sin Nature

Romans 8:9
But you are not controlled by your sinful nature. You are controlled by the Spirit if you have the Spirit of God living in you. (And remember that those who do not have the Spirit of Christ living in them do not belong to him at all.)

Paul declares that we do not have a sinful nature IF the Spirit of God lives in us. Then he says, "remember those who do not have the Spirit do not belong to Christ at all." This is very clear, we do not have two natures living in us at the same time as some would suggest. We are either saved or we are not. We either have a new nature or a sinful nature.

Colossians 2:11–12
When you came to Christ, you were "circumcised," but not by a physical procedure. Christ performed a spiritual

circumcision the cutting away of your sinful nature. For you were buried with Christ when you were baptized. And with him you were raised to new life because you trusted the mighty power of God, who raised Christ from the dead.

Colossians 3:9
Don't lie to each other, for you have stripped off your old sinful nature and all its wicked deeds.

Your Body Will Still Die

Romans 8:10–11
And Christ lives within you, so even though your body will die because of sin, the Spirit gives you life because you have been made right with God. The Spirit of God, who raised Jesus from the dead, lives in you. And just as God raised Christ Jesus from the dead, he will give life to your mortal bodies by this same Spirit living within you.

Here we must be careful that we don't get confused. All through this passage Paul has been contrasting the Holy Spirit and the sin nature, he uses the Greek word *sarx*, which refers to the body. Paul is talking about the physical body when he writes 'your body is dead'. Even if Christ is in you, your body will still go through death. Why? Because of sin. We must pay the temporal punishment for our sin. We must die. Death is the last enemy to be destroyed.

God raised up Jesus by the Holy Spirit. The Holy Spirit gave life to the body of Jesus in the tomb and affected his resurrection from the grave. Now listen to what Paul is saying: "If the Spirit of God, who raised Jesus from the dead, lives in you, then just as God raised Christ Jesus from the dead, he will give life to your mortal bodies by this same Spirit living within you." The same power that God used to raise Jesus from the dead is living inside believers right now. If you are a believer, your body will die because of sin, but it will be raised because the Holy Spirit lives in you.

We have no Obligation

Romans 8:12–14
Therefore, dear brothers and sisters, you have no obligation to do what your sinful nature urges you to do. For if you live by its dictates, you will die. But if through the power of the Spirit you put to death the deeds of your sinful nature, you will live. For all who are led by the Spirit of God are children of God.

Therefore! Because we have a new nature, because the Holy Spirit lives in us and will raise our mortal bodies, we have no obligation to do what the sinful nature urges us to do. We have a choice. Now that we have a new nature we are no longer under the control of the sin nature and therefore, do not have to obey it.

Our obligation does not require us to act on our own, independent of the work of the Spirit within us. It is our faith that must be exercised; we must work out our salvation in fear and trembling, but all this is in, by, and through the indwelling power of the Holy Spirit.

Romans 8:14
For all who are led by the Spirit of God are children of God.

Children of God

Romans 8:15–17
So, you have not received a spirit that makes you fearful slaves. Instead, you received God's Spirit when he adopted you as his own children. Now we call him, "Abba, Father." For his Spirit joins with our spirit to affirm that we are God's children. And since we are his children, we are his heirs. In fact, together with Christ we are heirs of God's glory. But if we are to share his glory, we must also share his suffering.

We received a spirit which frees us from fearful slavery. This is what is accomplished at justification by the indwelling of the Holy Spirit. When the Holy Spirit comes into our lives we receive the Spirit of adoption. God adopts us. By nature, we are now the children of God. The only way we can enter the family of God is to be adopted through our faith in Jesus Christ.

1 John 5:1
Everyone who believes that Jesus is the Christ has become a child of God. And everyone who loves the Father loves his children, too.

The Holy Spirit testifies, with our spirit that we are the children of God. The work of the Spirit gives us an inner assurance of our right standing with God. The Holy Spirit gives us confidence of our adoption into the family of God.

As family, we share in God's glory. Yet to share in his glory we must also share in suffering. This is a change in thought. I'm an heir of God and share in His glory. Wonderful! Now what is this suffering about?

CHESTER GROSS

Chapter 13

Future Glory

Romans 8:18–22
Yet what we suffer now is nothing compared to the glory he will reveal to us later. For all creation is waiting eagerly for that future day when God will reveal who his children really are. Against its will, all creation was subjected to God's curse. But with eager hope, the creation looks forward to the day when it will join God's children in glorious freedom from death and decay. For we know that all creation has been groaning as in the pains of childbirth right up to the present time.

From this point, Romans seems to move in a different

direction. While this seems to be the case it is not an entirely different direction but a parallel one. The first half of Romans, Paul blasts the Jewish people for their inability to keep the law and shows them that without faith it is impossible to please God. Circumcision no longer can make someone right with God, now it is the circumcision of the heart that matters.

Paul contrasts grace and the law with a sinful nature and a new nature. The sin nature which was to be governed by the law will not produce a glorious future. Heaven cannot be attained while someone still has a sinful nature. Nor, can the existence of a glorified body take place with a sinful nature.

Future glory speaks of natural redemption. For people, future glory is the glorification of the body and eternal life. Future glory for the earth is redemption from decay and corruption. A new heaven and earth.

When Adam fell the sin nature produced a curse. All of creation received a curse. Jesus as the second Adam reversed this curse. Yet, it is not completed, therefore the term future glory is used. Natural redemption still is incomplete. The earth still is cursed with decay and corruption. Man, still sweats, women still have pain in child bearing. The curse still exists and at the end of time the curse will be removed and all of creation will be redeemed.

Genesis 3:16–19
Then he said to the woman, "I will sharpen the pain of your pregnancy, and in pain you will give birth. And you will desire to control your husband, but he will rule over you." And to the man he said, "Since you listened to your wife and ate from the tree whose fruit I commanded you not to eat, the ground is cursed because of you. All your life you will struggle to scratch a living from it. It will grow thorns and thistles for you, though you will eat of its grains. By the sweat of your brow will you have food to eat until you return to the ground from which you were made. For you were made from dust, and to dust you will return."

Jesus redeemed all of creation from the curse brought through Adam. John the Revelator shares that when the new Jerusalem comes all nations will be healed and the curse will be removed.

Revelation 22:3
No longer will there be a curse upon anything. For the throne of God and of the Lamb will be there, and his servants will worship him.

Romans 8:23–25
And we believers also groan, even though we have the Holy Spirit within us as a foretaste of future glory, for we long for our bodies to be released from sin and suffering. We, too, wait with eager hope for the day when God will

give us our full rights as his adopted children, including the new bodies he has promised us. We were given this hope when we were saved. (If we already have something, we don't need to hope for it. But if we look forward to something we don't yet have, we must wait patiently and confidently.)

The Body Still Dies

Romans 8:10–11
And Christ lives within you, so even though your body will die because of sin, the Spirit gives you life because you have been made right with God. The Spirit of God, who raised Jesus from the dead, lives in you. And just as God raised Christ Jesus from the dead, he will give life to your mortal bodies by this same Spirit living within you.

Even though we have been redeemed from the curse of the sin nature death is still at work in us. First Corinthians says the death is the last enemy to be destroyed.

1 Corinthians 15:26
And the last enemy to be destroyed is death.

Salvation is a three-fold work. Justification is the exchange of a sinful nature to a new Christ nature. This comes through faith in the work of Jesus on the cross. Justification is a free gift from God. The second area is

Sanctification which is the renewal of the mind, will and emotions. Sanctification produces holiness and is our responsibility to work through. We must work out our own salvation. Third, is glorification this happens in the future glory. It is the glorification of our mortal bodies. Mortal becomes immortal. Glorification is the final work of salvation and does not happen until the end of time.

The Holy Spirit is our foretaste of the future glory which will be completed at the end of time when God brings all things under His Son, Jesus Christ. Then both mankind and the earth, are promised freedom from the curse of death.

Romans 8:23
And we believers also groan, even though we have the Holy Spirit within us as a foretaste of future glory, for we long for our bodies to be released from sin and suffering. We, too, wait with eager hope for the day when God will give us our full rights as his adopted children, including the new bodies he has promised us.

All creation groans looking toward the day when our bodies will be released from sin. We also look forward to the day when our bodies will become immortal. There is a desire in both the earth and mankind to see the completion of salvation which is to come.

Romans 8:24–25
We were given this hope when we were saved. (If we already have something, we don't need to hope for it. But if we look forward to something we don't yet have, we must wait patiently and confidently.)

1 Thessalonians 4:13–18
And now, dear brothers and sisters, we want you to know what will happen to the believers who have died so you will not grieve like people who have no hope. For since we believe that Jesus died and was raised to life again, we also believe that when Jesus returns, God will bring back with him the believers who have died. We tell you this directly from the Lord: We who are still living when the Lord returns will not meet him ahead of those who have died. For the Lord himself will come down from heaven with a commanding shout, with the voice of the archangel, and with the trumpet call of God. First, the believers who have died will rise from their graves. Then, together with them, we who are still alive and remain on the earth will be caught up in the clouds to meet the Lord in the air. Then we will be with the Lord forever. So encourage each other with these words.

Now that we have this hope we must wait for it. The completion of salvation will come at the appointed time. Our hope is that when Jesus returns all those who have died will return with Him and those whom are still alive will meet Him in the air and forever be with the Lord.

The Holy Spirit Helps Us

Romans 8:26–28
And the Holy Spirit helps us in our weakness. For example, we don't know what God wants us to pray for. But the Holy Spirit prays for us with groaning's that cannot be expressed in words. And the Father who knows all hearts knows what the Spirit is saying, for the Spirit pleads for us believers in harmony with God's own will. And we know that God causes everything to work together for the good of those who love God and are called according to his purpose for them.

The redemption of our bodies is the context of what we have been talking about. Now, Paul reminds us that the Holy Spirit helps us in our weakness. Weakness is defined as infirmity, disease or weakness of the body. Our bodies are still subject to death and decay. Sickness is a process which produces death in the body. The Holy Spirit helps us when our bodies are weak or sick.

Our example of the Holy Spirit's help is found in prayer. When we have no clue how to pray for our situation the Holy Spirit prays for us and the Father knows what our needs are. And, we know that God causes all things to work together for our good.

God Knew us in Advance

Romans 8:29–30
For God knew his people in advance, and he chose them to become like his Son, so that his Son would be the firstborn among many brothers and sisters. And having chosen them, he called them to come to him. And having called them, he gave them right standing with himself. And having given them right standing, he gave them his glory.

God is all knowing therefore, He knew His people before they were born and chose them to be like Jesus. Redemption was not plan B, God did not make a mistake. He was not surprised when Adam sinned. God knew before and had already planned for Jesus to die for the sin of humanity caused by Adam.

Ephesians 1:4
Even before he made the world, God loved us and chose us in Christ to be holy and without fault in his eyes.

God knew before the entrance of sin in the Garden of Eden, that man would fall. He is Omniscient (All Knowing). God foreknew that his creation would sin. Knowing this, God planned for this fall by sending his Son to die for his creation. We realize that Jesus did not come and die for man immediately following Adam's sin, but the Bible does tell us that Jesus planned to lay his life down for man before the world was created. Therefore, God's eternal plan would begin to unfold at the point of man's sin in the Garden of Eden.

Nothing Can Separate us from His Love

Romans 8:31–34
What shall we say about such wonderful things as these? If God is for us, who can ever be against us? Since he did not spare even his own Son but gave him up for us all, won't he also give us everything else? Who dares accuse us whom God has chosen for his own? No one for God himself has given us right standing with himself. Who then will condemn us? No one for Christ Jesus died for us and was raised to life for us, and he is sitting in the place of honor at God's right hand, pleading for us.

What should our response be to this announcement of Divine sovereignty working itself out in history for our redemption? Since God did not spare His Son won't He give us everything else? Future glory is not only our hope it is our guarantee. So, who can condemn us? No one! Because Jesus is sitting in the place of honor praying for us. What an incredible promise!

God Loves Us

Romans 8:35–39
Can anything ever separate us from Christ's love? Does it mean he no longer loves us if we have trouble or calamity, or are persecuted, or hungry, or destitute, or in danger, or threatened with death? (As the Scriptures say, "For your sake we are killed every day; we are being slaughtered like

sheep.") No, despite all these things, overwhelming victory is ours through Christ, who loved us. And I am convinced that nothing can ever separate us from God's love. Neither death nor life, neither angels nor demons, neither our fears for today nor our worries about tomorrow—not even the powers of hell can separate us from God's love. No power in the sky above or in the earth below—indeed, nothing in all creation will ever be able to separate us from the love of God that is revealed in Christ Jesus our Lord.

There is nothing which can condemn us nor separate us from the love of God. Here we stand before God, justified, having no condemnation to fear, with Christ as our Advocate. What is there in this world that can demolish or destroy the love Christ has for his people? In the rest of the chapter, Paul lists various things that could possibly separate us from the love of Christ.

Our context has been the weakness of the human body, it's ultimate redemption. Notice that all the things Paul lists are problems we face in our bodies. Calamity, hungry, destitute or danger.

After this first list of human problems Paul adds the spiritual problems. Demons, angels, worries, not even the powers of hell, nothing in all of creation has the power to stop God from loving us. We should be confident in God's love for us despite all the struggles we go through. So, we can be confident of God's plan for our future glory.

Chapter 14

The Jewish People

Romans 9:1–3
With Christ as my witness, I speak with utter truthfulness. My conscience and the Holy Spirit confirm it. My heart is filled with bitter sorrow and unending grief for my people, my Jewish brothers and sisters. I would be willing to be forever cursed cut off from Christ! if that would save them.

Paul affirmed his deep anguish of heart over the rejection of the gospel by the clear majority of Jews. His desire for their salvation was so strong that he was at the point of wishing that he were cursed and cut off from Christ for his kinsmen, the Israelites.

Seven Spiritual Advantages

Romans 9:4–5
They are the people of Israel, chosen to be God's adopted children. God revealed his glory to them. He made covenants with them and gave them his law. He gave them the privilege of worshiping him and receiving his wonderful promises. Abraham, Isaac, and Jacob are their ancestors, and Christ himself was an Israelite as far as his human nature is concerned. And he is God, the one who rules over everything and is worthy of eternal praise! Amen.

Paul lists seven spiritual privileges which Israel had been given over any other people group until now. God had made them his children and showed them His glory. Made covenants with them and gave them the law. They had the privilege to worship Him, they had linage from the line of Abraham and even Jesus was one of them. This list affirms the Jews promises and heritage.

They are God's Children through adoption. Glory was revealed to them through the pillar of a cloud and the fire at night as they were led out of Egypt. When the tabernacle in the wilderness was built, God filled it with His glory.

The covenant which was the basis for Israel's religious life was made at Mount Sinai. There are several covenants in scripture, it is the covenant given at Mount Sinai that brought the law. Paul next, referred to the linage of Abraham in chapter four, and now again asserts their relationship with God through their father Abraham. Lastly, the human part of Jesus was Jewish, Jesus was one of them.

Children of Promise

Romans 9:6–9
Well then, has God failed to fulfill his promise to Israel? No, for not all who are born into the nation of Israel are truly members of God's people! Being descendants of Abraham doesn't make them truly Abraham's children. For the Scriptures say, "Isaac is the son through whom your descendants will be counted," though Abraham had other children, too. This means that Abraham's physical descendants are not necessarily children of God. Only the children of the promise are considered to be Abraham's children. For God had promised, "I will return about this time next year, and Sarah will have a son."

The failure of the Jews to respond to the gospel of Christ did not mean God's Word had failed. Instead, this rejection was simply the example of the principle of God's sovereign choice established in the Old Testament. Paul reminded his readers of a truth he had presented earlier: For not all who are descended from Israel are Israel, that is, spiritual Israel.

The problem Paul has is that the Jews were certain of their future because of the covenant promises God had made. They had concluded that by the very fact of their birth into the nation of Israel, they were guaranteed all the promises of salvation. But Paul shows that it is not as though God's word had failed. God had promised to bless Israel but the point Paul makes is that not all who are descended from Israel are Israel. Nor because they are his descendants are they all Abraham's children.

In other words, it is not the natural children who are God's children, but it is the children of the promise who are regarded as Abraham's offspring. Abraham had more than one child: he had Ishmael as well as Isaac, but Ishmael did not receive the promise as Isaac did. God's promise is given sovereignly, not biologically.

Romans 9:10–16
This son was our ancestor Isaac. When he married Rebekah, she gave birth to twins. But before they were born, before they had done anything good or bad, she received a message from God. (This message shows that God chooses people according to his own purposes; he calls people, but not according to their good or bad works.) She was told, "Your older son will serve your younger son." In the words of the Scriptures, "I loved Jacob, but I rejected Esau." Are we saying, then, that God was unfair? Of course not! For God said to Moses, "I will show mercy to anyone I choose, and I will show

compassion to anyone I choose." So, it is God who decides to show mercy. We can neither choose it nor work for it.

The second illustration of God's sovereign choice is drawn from the second generation of Jewish ancestry. Apparently, God purposed to establish this principle clearly at the beginning of His relationship with His Chosen People. This illustration emphasizes God's sovereignty even more than the first since it involves God's choice of one twin over another. In the case of Abraham's sons, God chose the child of one woman over the child of another woman.

This story, as in that of Abraham, has to do with two brothers. Not only do they the same father; they have also have the same mother, and their origin goes back to the same moment of conception. The distinction between the twins is expressed between conception and birth.

Rebecca was informed, the older will serve the younger a divine choice confirmed by God's declaration; Jacob I loved, but Esau I hated. Esau, the older, did not actually serve Jacob, his younger twin; but Esau's descendants, the Edomite's, did. God's "love" for Jacob was revealed in His choice of Jacob and God's "hatred" for Esau was seen in His rejecting Esau for the line of promise. Hatred in this sense is not absolute but relative to a higher choice.

It does not depend on man's desire or effort, but on God's mercy. This verse should put an end to the debate forever. God could not make it any clearer. Salvation is by grace and by grace alone. God has mercy upon whom He chooses, we cannot work for it. God decides!

Romans 9:17–18
For the Scriptures say that God told Pharaoh, "I have appointed you for the very purpose of displaying my power in you and to spread my fame throughout the earth." So you see, God chooses to show mercy to some, and he chooses to harden the hearts of others so they refuse to listen.

The third illustration is Pharaoh. God had appointed him for the very purpose of displaying His power and to spread His fame throughout the earth. Which it clearly did, especially after Israel crossed the Jordan river and took the city of Jericho.

Romans 9:19–21
Well then, you might say, "Why does God blame people for not responding? Haven't they simply done what he makes them do?" No, don't say that. Who are you, a mere human being, to argue with God? Should the thing that was created say to the one who created it, "Why have you made me like this?" When a potter makes jars out of clay, doesn't he have a right to use the same lump of clay to make one jar for decoration and another to throw garbage

into?

Paul sums up his illustrations with a question. "Why does God still blame us?" Paul challenges the reader with the question, "who are you to talk back to God?" Paul rebukes his opponents by pointing out that their humanness does not give them the right to question God. The creation has no right to question the creator. God has the right to use His creation however He pleases.

Romans 9:22–29
In the same way, even though God has the right to show his anger and his power, he is very patient with those on whom his anger falls, who are destined for destruction. He does this to make the riches of his glory shine even brighter on those to whom he shows mercy, who were prepared in advance for glory. And we are among those whom he selected, both from the Jews and from the Gentiles. Concerning the Gentiles, God says in the prophecy of Hosea,

> "Those who were not my people,
>   I will now call my people.
> And I will love those
>   whom I did not love before."

And,

> "Then, at the place where they were told,
>   'You are not my people,'
> there they will be called

children of the living God.

And concerning Israel, Isaiah the prophet cried out,

> "Though the people of Israel are as numerous as the sand of the seashore,
> only a remnant will be saved.
> For the LORD will carry out his sentence upon the earth quickly and with finality."

And Isaiah said the same thing in another place:

> "If the LORD of Heaven's Armies
> had not spared a few of our children,
> we would have been wiped out like Sodom,
> destroyed like Gomorrah."

Here Paul quotes Old Testament verses to support the fact that God in His sovereign choice and calling, always includes a Jewish segment, though it is a minority. The passages quoted (Isa. 10:22–23 and 1:9), make it clear that in God's judgment on Israel He by sovereign choice preserves and saves a remnant. Those promises were fulfilled in the captivity and exile of both Israel and Judah and in the destruction of Jerusalem in A.D. 70 and will also be fulfilled in the national end-time deliverance of Israel (Rom. 11:26–27). Even today the same principle is true. Jews who become members of the church, the body of Christ, are what Paul later called "a remnant chosen by grace," which included himself.

Romans 9:30–33

What does all this mean? Even though the Gentiles were not trying to follow God's standards, they were made right with God. And it was by faith that this took place. But the people of Israel, who tried so hard to get right with God by keeping the law, never succeeded. Why not? Because they were trying to get right with God by keeping the law instead of by trusting in him. They stumbled over the great rock in their path. God warned them of this in the Scriptures when he said,

> "I am placing a stone in Jerusalem that makes people stumble,
> a rock that makes them fall.
> But anyone who trusts in him
> will never be disgraced."

It is by faith that the Gentiles could get right with God. Israel tried to get right with God by keeping the law, yet failed. Israel failed to trust God and therefore, stumbled over the rock in their way.

The Jews pursued righteousness, but they pursued it in exactly the opposite way that it is to be found. They pursued it in their own strength, by their own works, by their own merit, and consequently fell into a spirit of self-righteousness.

Christ came to his own people as a rock and a Savior. Instead of standing on the rock they tripped over the rock, and it became a stumbling-stone to them. With the appearance of Jesus, it was clear that there was only one way to get to heaven, namely, by exercising faith in Christ alone. That's what his contemporaries could not handle, because he was saying to them, 'Your works are not pure enough to merit entry into the kingdom of God. This infuriated them because the doctrine of justification by faith alone is a violent assault upon human pride. Instead of allowing Jesus to lift them up, they tripped over him. Chapter nine ends with this statement: and the one who trusts in him will never be put to shame.

Chapter 15

Salvation for Everyone

Romans 10:1–4
Dear brothers and sisters, the longing of my heart and my prayer to God is for the people of Israel to be saved. I know what enthusiasm they have for God, but it is misdirected zeal. For they don't understand God's way of making people right with himself. Refusing to accept God's way, they cling to their own way of getting right with God by trying to keep the law. For Christ has already accomplished the purpose for which the law was given. As a result, all who believe in him are made right with God.

Chapter nine started with Paul stating his concern for

his fellow Jews, and chapter ten begins in a similar way. He says, Brothers, my heart's desire and prayer to God for the Israelites is that they may be saved. He is still pouring out his personal anguish over the situation of his fellow kinsmen.

Paul's fellow Jews are zealous for God, but their zeal is not based on knowledge. There is a sense in which this verse is terrifying. Paul is describing people who are under the judgment of God, and yet have a zeal for God. The problem with their zeal for God was that it was based on bad theology. Israel neglected the truth of God and were slothful and indolent with respect to their study of the things of God.

Since they did not know the righteousness that comes from God and sought to establish their own, they did not submit to God's righteousness. God did not accept the Israelites because they put their faith in their own law-keeping, and not in the Savior. But Christ is the end of the law so that there may be righteousness for everyone who believes. The law which itself reveals the pattern of good works should drive us to Christ. Christ is the point of the law; Christ is the goal of the law; Christ is the meaning of the law. So, if you try to follow and obey the law, but avoid Christ, you have missed the whole point of the law.

Salvation for Everyone

Romans 10:5–11
For Moses writes that the law's way of making a person right with God requires obedience to all of its commands. But faith's way of getting right with God says, "Don't say in your heart, 'Who will go up to heaven?' (to bring Christ down to earth). And don't say, 'Who will go down to the place of the dead?' (to bring Christ back to life again)." In fact, it says, "The message is very close at hand; it is on your lips and in your heart." And that message is the very message about faith that we preach: If you openly declare that Jesus is Lord and believe in your heart that God raised him from the dead, you will be saved. For it is by believing in your heart that you are made right with God, and it is by openly declaring your faith that you are saved. As the Scriptures tell us, "Anyone who trusts in him will never be disgraced."

Paul further elaborates in verses five through seven, how Moses describes the righteousness that is by the law: "The man who does these things will live by them." But the righteousness that is by faith says: "Do not say in your heart, 'Who will ascend into heaven? (that is, to bring Christ down), "or 'Who will descend into the deep? (that is, to bring Christ up from the dead). This is difficult to understand.

There was a tradition among the Pharisees that if any single Pharisee kept all the Jewish laws perfectly for one day, that man's righteousness would be so pure that it would induce God to send the Messiah. The idea was that if a person was good enough he could have the merit to climb right up to heaven and bring the Messiah down, or if the Messiah had gone into hell, he could bring him back up. But who has that kind of righteousness, that kind of merit? We can't climb up into heaven and bring the Savior down. The whole point is that only God can send a Savior from heaven, and only God can bring one back from the dead. Only God can save you and that is where your faith must be.

The message is not the law, it is faith in Jesus Christ. If we openly declare that Jesus is the Lord and believe in our hearts that God raised Him from the dead, then we will be saved. Salvation only comes through belief and the open declaration of that faith.

John 3:3
Whoever believes in the Son has eternal life, but whoever rejects the Son will not see life, for God's wrath remains on them.

John 3:36
And anyone who believes in God's Son has eternal life. Anyone who doesn't obey the Son will never experience eternal life but remains under God's angry judgment."

There is only one way for us to be reconciled to God and it is through faith in Jesus Christ. Anyone who believes in Jesus will have eternal life and escape God judgement.

Romans 10:12–15
Jew and Gentile are the same in this respect. They have the same Lord, who gives generously to all who call on him. For "Everyone who calls on the name of the Lord will be saved." But how can they call on him to save them unless they believe in him? And how can they believe in him if they have never heard about him? And how can they hear about him unless someone tells them? And how will anyone go and tell them without being sent? That is why the Scriptures say, "How beautiful are the feet of messengers who bring good news!"

Salvation knows no nationality, race or culture. Jews and Gentiles are the same when it comes to salvation. God wants everyone to come to Him and has offered salvation to all who have faith. The message of the gospel must be heard for faith to be activated. The message must be sent, this is what Paul is doing. He is sharing the message of the Gospel to the world.

Romans 10:16–21
But not everyone welcomes the Good News, for Isaiah the prophet said, "Lord, who has believed our message?" So faith comes from hearing, that is, hearing the Good News about Christ. But I ask, have the people of Israel actually heard the message? Yes, they have: "The message has gone throughout the earth, and the words to all the

world." But I ask, did the people of Israel really understand? Yes, they did, for even in the time of Moses, God said, "I will rouse your jealousy through people who are not even a nation. I will provoke your anger through the foolish Gentiles." And later Isaiah spoke boldly for God, saying, "I was found by people who were not looking for me. I showed myself to those who were not asking for me." But regarding Israel, God said, "All day long I opened my arms to them, but they were disobedient and rebellious."

Paul made it clear that God's offer of righteousness by faith was given to everyone, Jews and Gentiles alike. His focus in this chapter, however, has been on the people of Israel and their response to that offer. Therefore, he wrote, not all the Israelites accepted the good news. This failure of the Jews to respond to the good news was true in Jesus' days on earth and in Paul's day as well.

Someone, might insist that the Jews were not given adequate opportunity to hear the message. So, Paul said, But I ask, did they not hear? He then quoted Psalm 19:4, concerning God's general revelation of heaven. Paul's obvious answer to his question is that Israel had ample opportunity by both general and special revelation to respond to God.

Paul anticipated another objection. Someone might argue, "Yes, Israel heard but she did not understand that

God purposed to offer righteousness by faith to all mankind, including Gentiles." So, Paul wrote, Again I ask did Israel not understand? His answer this time was from two Old Testament quotations, one by Moses and the second by Isaiah. Both verses share God's turning to the Gentiles, whom the Jews thought had no understanding. At the same time, God, has not withheld salvation from Jews. He has held out His hands, imploring them to return to Him.

Deuteronomy 32:21
They have roused my jealousy by worshiping things that are not God; they have provoked my anger with their useless idols. Now I will rouse their jealousy through people who are not even a people; I will provoke their anger through the foolish Gentiles.

Isaiah 65:1
The LORD says, "I was ready to respond, but no one asked for help. I was ready to be found, but no one was looking for me. I said, 'Here I am, here I am!' to a nation that did not call on my name.

Not everyone welcomes the message of the gospel. The prophets spoke concerning the gospel. Paul askes, "did Israel really understand?" YES, they did!

Moses spoke about the jealousy caused through God's acceptance of the Gentiles. Again, Isaiah spoke of God looking for people who were not looking for Him. All day long God opened His arms to Israel and they were disobedient and rebellious. God wants all people to be saved, but not all people will respond to Him.

Chapter 16

God's Mercy for Israel

At this point in Romans (chaps. 9–11) God's righteousness for people has been displayed primarily in Israel's rejecting Christ and rebelling against God, and in God's choosing the Gentiles. These themes continue in this chapter, but God's sovereign choice also involves His restoring Israel.

Chapter eleven focuses on the reason the Jewish people have been rejected and why the Gentiles have been included into the family tree.

Romans 11:1–6
I ask, then, has God rejected his own people, the nation of

Israel? Of course not! I myself am an Israelite, a descendant of Abraham and a member of the tribe of Benjamin. No, God has not rejected his own people, whom he chose from the very beginning. Do you realize what the Scriptures say about this? Elijah the prophet complained to God about the people of Israel and said, "Lord, they have killed your prophets and torn down your altars. I am the only one left, and now they are trying to kill me, too." And do you remember God's reply? He said, "No, I have 7,000 others who have never bowed down to Baal!" It is the same today, for a few of the people of Israel have remained faithful because of God's grace his undeserved kindness in choosing them. And since it is through God's kindness, then it is not by their good works. For in that case, God's grace would not be what it really is free and undeserved.

In chapter nine Paul asks several questions, he continues this process in chapter eleven. Did God reject His own people? Of course not. Paul uses himself as a proof. He himself is a descendant of Abraham and a member of the tribe of Benjamin. Second, Paul illustrates his point with Elijah. Even when it seemed all Israel had rejected God, there were seven thousand more who had not rejected God.

Romans 11:7–10
So this is the situation: Most of the people of Israel have not found the favor of God they are looking for so

earnestly. A few have the ones God has chosen but the hearts of the rest were hardened. As the Scriptures say,

> "God has put them into a deep sleep.
> To this day he has shut their eyes so they do not see,
> and closed their ears so they do not hear."

Likewise, David said,

> "Let their bountiful table become a snare,
> a trap that makes them think all is well.
> Let their blessings cause them to stumble,
> and let them get what they deserve.
> Let their eyes go blind so they cannot see,
> and let their backs be bent forever."

Paul then discussed the remnant chosen by grace out of Israel. The Jews sought to be accepted by God based on works and the righteousness of the Law. However, they were not accepted by God; only the elect were, because of God's sovereign choice by grace. The others were hardened. Hardening involves spiritual drowsiness, blindness, and deafness. The second quotation is from Psalm 69:22–23, which predicts the very things which should have been the source of blessing to Israel became the reason for their rejection of Jesus as the Messiah.

Romans 11:11–12
Did God's people stumble and fall beyond recovery? Of course not! They were disobedient, so God made salvation available to the Gentiles. But he wanted his own people to

become jealous and claim it for themselves. Now if the Gentiles were enriched because the people of Israel turned down God's offer of salvation, think how much greater a blessing the world will share when they finally accept it.

Israel did not fail to the point of no return. There is still a chance for Israel. There is no doubt that the Jews, or most of them, have stumbled and lost their place; the Gentiles are now coming into the Kingdom of God. But does this mean that they are now out of the race? Certainly not!

Two things happened because of Israel's stumble. First, the Gentiles would be offered salvation. Second, with God's acceptance of the Gentiles, Israel would become envious.

Romans 11:13–16
I am saying all this especially for you Gentiles. God has appointed me as the apostle to the Gentiles. I stress this, for I want somehow to make the people of Israel jealous of what you Gentiles have, so I might save some of them. For since their rejection meant that God offered salvation to the rest of the world, their acceptance will be even more wonderful. It will be life for those who were dead! And since Abraham and the other patriarchs were holy, their descendants will also be holy just as the entire batch of dough is holy because the portion given as an offering is holy. For if the roots of the tree are holy, the branches will

be, too.

Paul shifts to the Gentiles. He has been appointed to reach the Gentiles with the gospel. Paul wants the Jews to see what God is doing for the Gentiles to make Israel jealous and be saved. The Jews were the first fruits; they were dedicated to God. Gentile converts are the rest of the loaf, and they belong to God too. Israel is the roots of the tree; it was offered to God. Believers (Jews and Gentiles) are the branches, and the branches belong to God too. So, the Jews do not have any special privilege over the Gentiles who are brought in later.

Romans 11:17–18
But some of these branches from Abraham's tree some of the people of Israel have been broken off. And you Gentiles, who were branches from a wild olive tree, have been grafted in. So now you also receive the blessing God has promised Abraham and his children, sharing in the rich nourishment from the root of God's special olive tree. But you must not brag about being grafted in to replace the branches that were broken off. You are just a branch, not the root.

The tree is an olive tree. Olive trees are magnificent, particularly their root systems, and the trunk of the olive tree is massive, strong, and very beautiful. With these root systems, olive trees have great branches bearing fruit. The branches, that were not bearing fruit, were cut off. But the tree was not left in that condition, or it would be disfigured and become stunted in its growth. God's work is not merely to cultivate by cutting off the dead branches, but by grafting new branches onto the tree. Paul says, a wild olive shoot has been joined to it.

Who are the wild olive branches? The Gentiles! They were strangers and foreigners to the covenant of God. They came out of paganism, wild olive trees, and they have been grafted in. Notice, God does not cut down the tree and plant a new tree. God doesn't do that; He keeps the substance of the tree and grafts on wild olive branches.

Jesus frequently spoke about bearing fruit. Jesus even cursed a fig tree for not producing fruit. Anyone who does not produce fruit will be cut off by the Father.

John 15:1–2
"I am the true grapevine, and my Father is the gardener. He cuts off every branch of mine that doesn't produce fruit, and he prunes the branches that do bear fruit so they will produce even more.

Romans 11:19–21
"Well," you may say, "those branches were broken off to make room for me." Yes, but remember those branches were broken off because they didn't believe in Christ, and you are there because you do believe. So, don't think

highly of yourself, but fear what could happen. For if God, did not spare the original branches, he won't spare you either.

Paul is still talking to the Gentiles and warning them to beware. Remember the branches were broken off because they did not believe in Christ and you Gentiles are there because you do believe in Christ. So, be careful how you think and do not allow pride in. If God did not spare the nation of Israel His own people, then He won't spare the Gentiles either.

Romans 11:22–24
Notice how God is both kind and severe. He is severe toward those who disobeyed, but kind to you if you continue to trust in his kindness. But if you stop trusting, you also will be cut off. And if the people of Israel turn from their unbelief, they will be grafted in again, for God has the power to graft them back into the tree. You, by nature, were a branch cut from a wild olive tree. So, if God was willing to do something contrary to nature by grafting you into his cultivated tree, he will be far more eager to graft the original branches back into the tree where they belong.

In these verses, Paul summarized his whole discussion of God's sovereign choice in temporarily putting Israel aside corporately and proclaiming righteousness by faith to all mankind.

God's choice involved severity toward the Jews who stumbled in unbelief and were hardened, but that same decision displayed the goodness of God toward individual Gentiles. God's continuing goodness to the Gentiles depends on their continuing in His kindness. If the Gentiles do not continue in God's kindness, they also will be cut off.

If the people of Israel, do not persist in unbelief, they will be grafted back in. God chose to put Israel aside corporately because of unbelief and to extend righteousness by faith to everyone. This demonstrates His decision to graft Gentiles into the spiritual linage of Abraham.

Salvation is for Everyone

Romans 11:25–27
I want you to understand this mystery, dear brothers and sisters, so that you will not feel proud about yourselves. Some of the people of Israel have hard hearts, but this will last only until the full number of Gentiles comes to Christ. And so, all Israel will be saved. As the Scriptures say,

> "The one who rescues will come from Jerusalem,
> 	and he will turn Israel away from ungodliness.
> And this is my covenant with them,
> 	that I will take away their sins."

God purposed people from all nations should by faith receive the righteousness provided by grace. To achieve this goal Israel's relationship as God's chosen people was rescinded for a time and Israel is now experiencing a hardening in part until the full number of the Gentiles has come in.

Acts 15:13–15
When they had finished, James stood and said, "Brothers, listen to me. Peter has told you about the time God first visited the Gentiles to take from them a people for himself. And this conversion of Gentiles is exactly what the prophets predicted.

Paul does not mean every Jew that ever lived, but the nation of Israel. All through his discussion Paul is talking about Israel in part. A part of Israel has been blinded, part of Israel has been cut away, part of Israel has been excluded from the kingdom of God and its blessings. The Jews as a people are presently under judgment. But as there was a national judgment, so there will be a national restoration. Their rejection, even though it was a national rejection, did not include the rejection of every individual. So, the restoration doesn't necessarily mean that every individual Jew will be saved, but the nation as a nation will be restored to God and believe in Christ Jesus as the Messiah.

Romans 11:28–36
Many of the people of Israel are now enemies of the Good News, and this benefits you Gentiles. Yet they are still the

people he loves because he chose their ancestors Abraham, Isaac, and Jacob. For God's gifts and his call can never be withdrawn. Once, you Gentiles were rebels against God, but when the people of Israel rebelled against him, God was merciful to you instead. Now they are the rebels, and God's mercy has come to you so that they, too, will share in God's mercy. For God, has imprisoned everyone in disobedience so he could have mercy on everyone. Oh, how great are God's riches and wisdom and knowledge! How impossible it is for us to understand his decisions and his ways!

> For who can know the LORD's thoughts?
>> Who knows enough to give him advice?
> And who has given him so much
>> that he needs to pay it back?

For everything comes from him and exists by his power and is intended for his glory. All glory to him forever! Amen.

The Gospel was preached to the Jews, and they rejected it, placing themselves under God's wrath, since the law, which they preferred to the way of faith, produces wrath. Their rejection of the Gospel, however, led to the mission to the Gentiles, and thereby turned out to be to the advantage of the Gentiles.

All things were created by God; all things exist through him; all things exist for him. He is the Creator of everyone and of all things, and all things exist by his power and through his power.

Acts 17:26–28
From one man he created all the nations throughout the whole earth. He decided beforehand when they should rise and fall, and he determined their boundaries. "His purpose was for the nations to seek after God and perhaps feel their way toward him and find him though he is not far from any one of us. For in him we live and move and exist. As some of your own poets have said, 'We are his offspring.'

God in His sovereignty determined the rise and the fall of every nation. His purpose was that nations would seek Him and find Him. There is a purpose to what God is doing. And we must not forget He is the creator and we are His creation. God knows what is best for every nation and every person.

CHESTER GROSS

Chapter 17

Transformation

Romans 12:1–2
And so, dear brothers and sisters, I plead with you to give your bodies to God because of all he has done for you. Let them be a living and holy sacrifice the kind he will find acceptable. This is truly the way to worship him. Don't copy the behavior and customs of this world, but let God transform you into a new person by changing the way you think. Then you will learn to know God's will for you, which is good and pleasing and perfect.

Let's step back and look at the last verse of chapter eleven. Paul is continuing his thought that everything exists by God's power and is intended for His glory.

Romans 11:36
For everything comes from him and exists by his power and is intended for his glory. All glory to him forever! Amen.

Considering everything exists by God's power and for His glory, we should present our natural bodies as a living holy sacrifice. Chapter six and eight both talked about living holy. We can now become holy because we have a new Spirit nature. Paul has told us that if we present our bodies over to the passions of the sin nature we will die, but if we allow the Holy Spirit to lead us we will have life and peace.

Later in this chapter Paul begins to discuss the gifts within the body of Christ and how each believer has a unique gift and purpose to fill in Christ's body.

True Worship

Offering our bodies as a living sacrifice is truly the way to worship him. When we give our bodies as a living sacrifice that is considered true worship. The word "worship" here is not the normal word used for worship which means to revere, praise and glorify God. This Greek word means to serve God with our bodies through acts of holiness. Giving our bodies as a sacrifice is acceptable and well pleasing to God. To live holy in our physical lives is the best way to serve God.

Next, we are warned not to copy the behavior and customs of the world around us. Behavior and customs is the same Greek word which means, to be conformed to the morals of the world system.

Galatians 1:4
Jesus gave his life for our sins, just as God our Father planned, in order to rescue us from this evil world in which we live.

Ephesians 2:2
You used to live in sin, just like the rest of the world, obeying the devil the commander of the powers in the unseen world. He is the spirit at work in the hearts of those who refuse to obey God.

Allow God to Transform You

Transformed is to become changed in outward appearance or expression as manifesting a change in your physical body. The Holy Spirit is mentioned only four times from chapter one through chapter seven, then twenty-two times in chapter eight. The Holy Spirit is the one who transforms us from the inside out. Once we have a new spirit nature the Holy Spirit regenerates our spirit man or heart and makes us a new creation, a new person. Paul concluded in chapter eight that those who are led by the Holy Spirit are the children of God.

The word, "transformed" is used only a few times in scripture, every other time it is used it refers to Jesus being transformed. At Gethsemane Jesus was transformed.

Matthew 17:2
As the men watched, Jesus' appearance was transformed so that his face shone like the sun, and his clothes became as white as light.

Transformed in our Thinking

Romans 12:2
Don't copy the behavior and customs of this world, but let God transform you into a new person by changing the way you think. Then you will learn to know God's will for you, which is good and pleasing and perfect.

We are transformed physically when we change the way we think. The new nature defeats the power and control of the sin nature, yet our minds still remember the behaviors of that nature. To be fully transformed we must change the way we think and put on the mind of Christ and think like Jesus would think.

This is where the process of sanctification begins.

Righteousness is a work of the spirit. Sanctification is the process of holiness. It is a work in the soul, the mind, will and emotions. With a new nature, we must now present our bodies as a living sacrifice and be renewed in the way we think.

The law only controlled the physical body, it could not change the heart or mind of people. Therefore, it was found with fault and removed. Now that we have a new nature in our spirit, our spirit with the Holy Spirit direct our minds, then our minds directs our bodies. Therefore, we can change since we have a new nature.

To know God's will, what is good and pleasing to Him we must learn how to think the way God thinks. Paul also told us to put on the mind of Christ. To be renewed in our minds. Then we can know the will of God for our lives.

Ephesians 4:22–24
Throw off your old sinful nature and your former way of life, which is corrupted by lust and deception. Instead, let the Spirit renew your thoughts and attitudes. Put on your new nature, created to be like God truly righteous and holy.

Colossians 1:21
This includes you who were once far away from God. You were his enemies, separated from him by your evil thoughts and actions.

Philippians 4:8
And now, dear brothers and sisters, one final thing. Fix your thoughts on what is true, and honorable, and right, and pure, and lovely, and admirable. Think about things that are excellent and worthy of praise.

2 Corinthians 10:3–5
We are human, but we don't wage war as humans do. We use God's mighty weapons, not worldly weapons, to knock down the strongholds of human reasoning and to destroy false arguments. We destroy every proud obstacle that keeps people from knowing God. We capture their rebellious thoughts and teach them to obey Christ.

The thoughts of the sinful nature separated us from God. Now we must allow the Holy Spirit to renew our thoughts, and begin to think the right way. Philippians says, "to think on these things," then gives us a list of the things we should think about. In Second Corinthians, the way in which we wage war is by capturing thoughts which are not in line with the Holy Spirit. This is how we will be transformed, renewed and sanctified. This is the process which produces holiness in us.

Thinking Right

Romans 12:3–5
Because of the privilege and authority God has given me, I give each of you this warning: Don't think you are better

than you really are. Be honest in your evaluation of yourselves, measuring yourselves by the faith God has given us. Just as our bodies have many parts and each part has a special function, so it is with Christ's body. We are many parts of one body, and we all belong to each other.

If we want to keep things in perspective, there are two things that we always must remember. We must remember first who God is, and second, we must remember who we are. If we really know who God is, it should not be too difficult to figure out who we are. Knowing that we are utterly dependent on grace for any achievement that we enjoy in this world, how can we be anything but humble. This verse prohibits pride and arrogance, a boastful exalted opinion of ourselves.

1 John 2:16
For the world offers only a craving for physical pleasure, a craving for everything we see, and pride in our achievements and possessions. These are not from the Father, but are from this world.

Chapter 18

Gifting's in the Body

Romans 12:4–8
Just as our bodies have many parts and each part has a special function, so it is with Christ's body. We are many parts of one body, and we all belong to each other. In his grace, God has given us different gifts for doing certain things well. So, if God has given you the ability to prophesy, speak out with as much faith as God has given you. If your gift is serving others, serve them well. If you are a teacher, teach well. If your gift is to encourage others, be encouraging. If it is giving, give generously. If God has given you leadership ability, take the responsibility seriously. And if you have a gift for showing

kindness to others, do it gladly.

Our body has many parts, each part has a special function which is different from the other parts. So it is in the family of God, the body of Christ. Every believer has been given a special gift by which they can serve God and people. These gifts enable and equip the believer for works of service. As Paul stated in verse two, our worship is serving.

One of the things we must understand is that whatever your gifting's are in the body of Christ they are worthy of development. We cannot minimize that gift. I was recently with a couple from the church. They were looking at homes, all very expensive homes. As we were looking at a house the wife kept saying, "I feel like God wants us to entertain a lot," so, I'm looking for a house where we can fit lots of people in. This is the gift of Hospitality. Years later I have been to countless events at their house.

Ephesians 4:15-16
Instead, we will speak the truth in love, growing in every way more and more like Christ, who is the head of his body, the church. He makes the whole body fit together perfectly. As each part does its own special work, it helps the other parts grow, so that the whole body is healthy and growing and full of love.

We realize that, as members of His body and a local church body, we belong to each other, we affect each other, and we need each other. Each believer, no matter how insignificant they may appear, have a ministry to other believers. The body grows as the individual members grow, and they grow as they feed on the Word of God and minister to each other. Note once again the emphasis on love: "forbearing one another in love" (Eph. 4:2); "speaking the truth in love" (Eph. 4:15); "the edifying of itself in love" (4:16). Love is the circulatory system of the body. It has been discovered that isolated, unloved babies do not grow properly and are especially susceptible to disease, while babies who are loved and touched grow normally and are stronger. So, it is with the children of God. An isolated Christian cannot minister to others, nor can others minister to him, and it is impossible for the gifts to be ministered in that way.

Romans 12:9-10
Don't just pretend to love others. Really love them. Hate what is wrong. Hold tightly to what is good. Love each other with genuine affection, and take delight in honoring each other.

Romans 13:8
Owe nothing to anyone except for your obligation to love one another. If you love your neighbor, you will fulfill the requirements of God's law.

Prophecy

Romans 12:6
In his grace, God has given us different gifts for doing certain things well. So if God has given you the ability to prophesy, speak out with as much faith as God has given you.

This word "Prophecy" in the Greek is used fifty-eight times in the New Testament. It means preaching the message of God, an inspired message or utterance; intelligible preaching, an intelligible message (as opposed to speaking in tongues). Not always prediction, but a speaking forth of God's message under the guidance of the Holy Spirit.

Prophecy is the ability to deliver inspired words which convey God's special message to the hearers. This could be seen in a pastor or speaker who receives an inspired word from God and speaks it out to people.

1 Corinthians 12:10
He gives one person the power to perform miracles, and another the ability to prophesy. He gives someone else the ability to discern whether a message is from the Spirit of God or from another spirit. Still another person is given the ability to speak in unknown languages, while another is given the ability to interpret what is being said.

Service

Romans 12:7
If your gift is serving others, serve them well. If you are a teacher, teach well.

The gift of service is the ability to identify and meet the practical needs of others. The word always appears in the New Testament about the service of the Christian church. The Greek word for servant or ministry is also used to describe a deacon. This word represents the servant in his activity. The word therefore refers to one who serves.

The one who serves must develop his gift of serving. Those who serve should render service in the realm in which God placed them and for which He gave them that gift.

Ephesians 6:7–8
Work with enthusiasm, as though you were working (serving) for the Lord rather than for people. Remember that the Lord will reward each one of us for the good we do, whether we are slaves or free.

Serving simply is helping meet the needs of people. The gift of service cares about people and naturally wants to help them. These people will always come to your aid to help you do just about anything.

Teacher

Romans 12:7
If your gift is serving others, serve them well. If you are a teacher, teach well.

The gift of teaching is the ability to employ a logical, systematic approach to biblical study in preparation for clearly communicating practical truth to the body of Christ. The one who is given a teaching gift should remain within the exercise of that gift. It is a wise man who stays within the sphere of service for which God the Holy Spirit has fitted him, and does not invade some other field of service for which he is not fitted.

Here the scripture says that if a person's gift is teaching let him teach. The word teach is used twice but they are two different Greek words.

The first one defines a teacher as one who instructs and imparts understanding. The second one, means he who teaches must continually learn. Anyone wanting to be a teacher must be a learner who studies the scriptures and the precepts of God.

Encouragement

Romans 12:8
If your gift is to encourage others, be encouraging. If it is

giving, give generously. If God has given you leadership ability, take the responsibility seriously. And if you have a gift for showing kindness to others, do it gladly.

Encouragement is a gift which uses words. It is the act of supporting or encouraging someone. Encouragement can take several forms, to exhort, to comfort and to build up someone with words of affirmation.

Ephesians 4:29
Don't use foul or abusive language. Let everything you say be good and helpful, so that your words will be an encouragement to those who hear them.

Giving

Romans 12:8
If your gift is to encourage others, be encouraging. If it is giving, give generously. If God has given you leadership ability, take the responsibility seriously. And if you have a gift for showing kindness to others, do it gladly.

The gift of giving is the willingness to contribute money and resources to the Lord's work with cheerfulness and generosity. This gift gives beyond normal giving. It is a gift that gives without being pressured.

2 Corinthians 8:7
Since you excel in so many ways in your faith, your gifted

speakers, your knowledge, your enthusiasm, and your love from us I want you to excel also in this gracious act of giving.

People with the gift of giving manage their finances well. They are disciplined when it comes to money, yet have a heart for meeting people's needs with their resources. They are generous to a fault, they like to give without being seen. They give when no one else gives. They are givers by nature, most likely started when they were children.

Just yesterday a family member passed away. Another family member heard about it and within minutes of hearing, offered to buy five airplane tickets for the immediate family to travel across country to be there for the funeral. This is clearly the gift of giving.

Leadership

Romans 12:8
If your gift is to encourage others, be encouraging. If it is giving, give generously. If God has given you leadership ability, take the responsibility seriously. And if you have a gift for showing kindness to others, do it gladly.

Leadership is to lead or direct people with the desire to care for them and help them. Leaders motivate and direct people to accomplish God's purposes. As in all the gifts, leaders tend to become leaders naturally. Most have been thrust into leadership positions most of their lives. It comes natural for them to lead others. They provide guidance and vision. Leaders also equip and train people in the task they are leading. A good leader leads by example setting the standard of leadership by their lifestyle. People naturally follow them.

1 Corinthians 12:28 "Here are some of the parts God has appointed for the church: first are apostles, second are prophets, third are teachers, then those who do miracles, those who have the gift of healing, those who can help others, those who have the gift of leadership, those who speak in unknown languages."

Kindness (Mercy)

Romans 12:8
If your gift is to encourage others, be encouraging. If it is giving, give generously. If God has given you leadership ability, take the responsibility seriously. And if you have a gift for showing kindness to others, do it gladly.

Kindness is also the word mercy. It means to be patient and compassionate toward those who are suffering or afflicted. The concern for the physical as well as the spiritual needs of those who are hurting is covered by the gift of kindness. Those with this gift have great empathy for others in their trials and sufferings. They can come alongside people over extended periods of time and see them through their healing process. They are truly and literally the hands and feet of God to the afflicted.

The Holy Spirit gives the spiritual gift of kindness to people in the church to love and assist those who are suffering. Those with this gift are able to "weep with those who weep", and "bear one another's burdens". They are sensitive to the feelings and circumstances of others and can quickly discern when someone is hurting.

Colossians 3:12
Since God chose you to be the holy people he loves, you must clothe yourselves with tenderhearted mercy, kindness, humility, gentleness, and patience.

God builds His church as he chooses, He assigns each person their part in His body. We don't get to choose which part we want to be. It is God who adds to the church and chooses which part each person will become.

1 Corinthians 12:24–26
While the more honorable parts do not require this special care. So God has put the body together such that extra honor and care are given to those parts that have less dignity. This makes for harmony among the members, so that all the members care for each other. If one part suffers, all the parts suffer with it, and if one part is honored, all the parts are glad.

The parts of the body which seem insignificant God gives more honor. If the toe is broken it effects the entire body. The foot and leg must work harder to make up for the weakness in the toe. If one part suffers all the parts suffer.

God has made the body to become more and more like Christ. As each part of the body does what it is called to do, the church will increase and be strong. Therefore, it is important for the ministry leaders to equip the saints. If the saints are not equipped to know their place and role in the body of Christ, they will not function properly or not all.

1 Peter 4:10–11
"God has given each of you a gift from his great variety of spiritual gifts. Use them well to serve one another. Do you have the gift of speaking? Then speak as though God himself were speaking through you. Do you have the gift of helping others? Do it with all the strength and energy that God supplies. Then everything you do will bring glory to God through Jesus Christ. All glory and power to him forever and ever! Amen."

Chapter 19

Really Love People

Romans 12:9–13
Don't just pretend to love others. Really love them. Hate what is wrong. Hold tightly to what is good. Love each other with genuine affection, and take delight in honoring each other. Never be lazy, but work hard and serve the Lord enthusiastically. Rejoice in our confident hope. Be patient in trouble, and keep on praying. When God's people are in need, be ready to help them. Always be eager to practice hospitality.

Don't pretend to love each other. Pretend is the word hypocrite. It means don't hide behind a mask which looks like love but underneath really doesn't care. Really love people, Paul uses the word, 'agape" here which is to love by an act of ones will, deciding to love whether you feel like it or not. Love here is a choice, I decide if I am going to love people or not.

Galatians 5:6
For when we place our faith in Christ Jesus, there is no benefit in being circumcised or being uncircumcised. What is important is faith expressing itself in love.

Verse ten says to love each other with genuine affection, to really care about people, to be happy to honor them. Honor means to give respect to people.

1 John 3:18–19
Dear children, let's not merely say that we love each other; let us show the truth by our actions. Our actions will show that we belong to the truth, so we will be confident when we stand before God.

Never be Lazy

Romans 12:11
Never be lazy, but work hard and serve the Lord enthusiastically.

Love is never lazy, it is always willing to help people and serve the Lord. Love always seeks to help people, it is caring and kind.

Rejoice in Hope

Romans 12:12–13
Rejoice in our confident hope. Be patient in trouble, and keep on praying. When God's people are in need, be ready to help them. Always be eager to practice hospitality.

We are to be joyful in hope. Our hope is found in the future glory promised us through Jesus Christ.

Be Patient in Troubles

Romans 12:12–13
Rejoice in our confident hope. Be patient in trouble, and keep on praying. When God's people are in need, be ready to help them. Always be eager to practice hospitality.

Troubles are problems we face in life. We all have troubles we all struggle with pressures in life. Paul exhorts us to be patient in our troubles. Patience means to endure or remain under the pressure.

2 Corinthians 6:4
In everything we do, we show that we are true ministers of God. We patiently endure troubles and hardships and calamities of every kind.

1 Peter 1:6–7
So be truly glad. There is wonderful joy ahead, even though you must endure many trials for a little while. These trials will show that your faith is genuine. It is being tested as fire tests and purifies gold though your faith is far more precious than mere gold. So, when your faith remains strong through many trials, it will bring you much praise and glory and honor on the day when Jesus Christ is revealed to the whole world.

Continue in Prayer

Romans 12:12–13
Rejoice in our confident hope. Be patient in trouble, and keep on praying. When God's people are in need, be ready to help them. Always be eager to practice hospitality.

We must not give up praying when we are under pressure and enduring troubles. Prayer is effectual when we continue to press through.

1 Thessalonians 5:16–18
Always be joyful. Never stop praying. Be thankful in all circumstances, for this is God's will for you who belong to Christ Jesus.

Help People in Need

Romans 12:12–13
Rejoice in our confident hope. Be patient in trouble, and keep on praying. When God's people are in need, be ready to help them. Always be eager to practice hospitality.

Helping people in need should be normal for those who are followers of Christ. Scripture speaks frequently about loving each other, being kind, overlooking each other faults. Seeing a need and helping should be a normal action for believers.

Show Hospitality

Romans 12:12–13
Rejoice in our confident hope. Be patient in trouble, and keep on praying. When God's people are in need, be ready to help them. Always be eager to practice hospitality.

Hospitality is another virtue which every Christian must practice. After more than forty years in ministry I have rarely been invited to a church member's home. Even more rare was to be invited to a staff members house. My wife and I open our home frequently and intentionally. We believe it is extremely important for people to connect to each other and to us as pastors.

In Seattle, Starbucks has created a new culture. With coffee shops everywhere, hospitality is not limited to someone's home. There are different clubs which meet in coffee shops, business meetings and fellowship which take place over coffee. A coffee shop now in Seattle has replaced the way hospitality can connect people together.

Hebrews 13:2
Don't forget to show hospitality to strangers, for some who have done this have entertained angels without realizing it!

Bless those who Persecute

Romans 12:14
Bless those who persecute you. Don't curse them; pray that God will bless them.

The word for 'blessing' is the same word from which we get the English word, *eulogy*. To say something good about one who has persecuted us, takes as much grace as any virtue ever did, because our natural human tendency is to get even.

To curse others does not mean simply to insult them, it is to wish that God consigns them to unmitigated wrath and punishment for ever in hell. For any to wish for the damnation of another soul is an unthinkable grievance against the grace of God.

1 Corinthians 4:12
We work wearily with our own hands to earn our living.

We bless those who curse us. We are patient with those who abuse us.

Be Happy with others Happiness

Romans 12:15
Be happy with those who are happy, and weep with those who weep.

It takes real sensitivity, real grace and discipline to listen and watch for the moods of other people, and to express empathy. Empathy means to feel with another person. Paul is not referring to sympathy, but empathy, where we enter the feelings of others.

Live in Harmony

Romans 12:16
Live in harmony with each other. Don't be too proud to enjoy the company of ordinary people. And don't think you know it all!

Living in harmony doesn't mean we are always going to agree with everybody that we meet, but there is a way to handle disagreement. We must seek unity and try to find that place where we can come together. And even if we do disagree, we should have a good attitude.

We must be willing to associate with everyone, no

matter what their economic, ethnic or cultural background is. Christians must not be snobs. ALSO, don't think you know it all. You don't!

Never pay back Evil Live in Peace

Romans 12:17–18
Never pay back evil with more evil. Do things in such a way that everyone can see you are honorable. Do all that you can to live in peace with everyone.

There is never any justification for fighting evil with evil. Just because somebody treats you in an evil manner does not justify a response in kind. We are not to return evil for evil, but must return good for evil. We never have the right to do wrong, never have the right to do evil. Our obligation is to do what is right. We never pay back evil for evil, but we should live in peace with everyone.

Never take Revenge

Romans 12:19–21
Dear friends, never take revenge. Leave that to the righteous anger of God. For the Scriptures say, "I will take revenge; I will pay them back," says the LORD. Instead, "If your enemies are hungry, feed them. If they are thirsty, give them something to drink. In doing this, you will heap burning coals of shame on their heads. "Don't let evil conquer you, but conquer evil by doing good.

Never pay back wrong done to you out of vicious spite; wanting God to punish them for what they did to you. Instead we must turn to God. It is His right to judge not ours. Our response is to feed our enemy if they are hungry. The point is that whatever our enemy needs, if we can meet that need we should.

The coals on the head may refer to a ritual in Egypt in which a person showed his repentance by carrying a pan of burning charcoal on his head. Helping rather than cursing an enemy may cause him to be ashamed and repentant. As Paul summarized, do not be overcome by evil, giving in to the temptation to retaliate, but overcome evil with good.

Chapter twelve has been very practical. From being transformed to understanding our place and gifting's in the body, to exhortations to love each other and practical ways to show that love to others even our enemies. This chapter has given us a lot to work on.

Up to this point we have learned much about our new nature. Now we learn how a new nature acts in daily life and towards God and people. It's time to start the process of transformation!

Chapter 20

Governing Authority

Romans 13:1–7
Everyone must submit to governing authorities. For all authority comes from God, and those in positions of authority have been placed there by God. So, anyone who rebels against authority is rebelling against what God has instituted, and they will be punished. For the authorities do not strike fear in people who are doing right, but in those who are doing wrong. Would you like to live without fear of the authorities? Do what is right, and they will honor you. The authorities are God's servants, sent for your good. But if you are doing wrong, of course you should be afraid, for they have the power to punish you.

They are God's servants, sent for the very purpose of punishing those who do what is wrong. So you must submit to them, not only to avoid punishment, but also to keep a clear conscience. Pay your taxes, too, for these same reasons. For government workers need to be paid. They are serving God in what they do. Give to everyone what you owe them: Pay your taxes and government fees to those who collect them, and give respect and honor to those who are in authority.

Rome was the capital, the seat of the Roman empire's civil government. As residents of Rome, the readers would have been aware of the civil laws. But they were also citizens of Christ's kingdom. Appropriately, therefore, Paul discussed a Christian's relationship to his government and civil rulers.

Paul's exhortation is; everyone must submit to governing authorities. The basic reason for submission is that those authorities are established by God. An individual who rebels against the authority, is rebelling against God and what He has instituted. Those who obey and do right need have no fear of authorities; in fact, civil leaders commend those who do good.

Titus 3:1
Remind the believers to submit to the government and its officers. They should be obedient, always ready to do what is good.

1 Peter 2:13–14
For the Lord's sake, submit to all human authority whether the king as head of state, or the officials he has appointed. For the king has sent them to punish those who do wrong and to honor those who do right.

A civil leader is God's servant, a concept often forgotten today. By commending those who do right, a civil leader himself does good. But on the other hand, he has authority from God to punish wrong doing. A Christian has two reasons to be submissive to civil authorities. One, to avoid possible punishment and two, to heed his conscience, which encourages him to obey God's commands.

A Christian's responsibility to civil authorities involves more than obedience. It also includes support by paying taxes. This is because the leaders, as God's servants, are supposed to give their full time to governing and need support through taxes from citizens, Christians included. So a Christian ought to give everyone what he owes him, whether taxes or respect or honor. God set up the same system that He set up for the priests and those who minister. Israel was to tithe a tenth of their income so the priests could give themselves to full time ministry.

Love Fulfills God's Requirements

Romans 13:8–10
Owe nothing to anyone except for your obligation to love one another. If you love your neighbor, you will fulfill the requirements of God's law. For the commandments say, "You must not commit adultery. You must not murder. You must not steal. You must not covet." These and other such commandments are summed up in this one commandment: "Love your neighbor as yourself." Love does no wrong to others, so love fulfills the requirements of God's law.

Paul goes back to the ten commandments these given to Israel on Mt. Sinai. Here he lists the six commandments which relate to people rather than God. These six commandments are summed up into one single commandment. Love each other.

The other four commandments regarded our relationship with God which were also summed up in a single commandment. Love God with all your heart, soul, mind and strength.

In the New Covenant all ten commandments are summed up into two laws. Love God and love people. This is the only way that the ten commandments can ever be fully obeyed.

Matthew 22:37–40
Jesus replied, " 'You must love the Lord your God with all

your heart, all your soul, and all your mind.' This is the first and greatest commandment. A second is equally important: 'Love your neighbor as yourself.' The entire law and all the demands of the prophets are based on these two commandments."

The way we fulfill the ten commandments is through love for God and people. Love motivates obedience because no one wants to hurt the person they love. Love does no wrong to people. Therefore, love fulfills all the requirements of God and the law.

Time is Running Out

Romans 13:11–14
This is all the more urgent, for you know how late it is; time is running out. Wake up, for our salvation is nearer now than when we first believed. The night is almost gone; the day of salvation will soon be here. So, remove your dark deeds like dirty clothes, and put on the shining armor of right living. Because we belong to the day, we must live decent lives for all to see. Don't participate in the darkness of wild parties and drunkenness, or in sexual promiscuity and immoral living, or in quarreling and jealousy. Instead, clothe yourself with the presence of the Lord Jesus Christ. And don't let yourself think about ways to indulge your evil desires.

It's time to wake up. Paul thought Christ's return

could occur at any time. Paul said, we are closer than ever before. When Jesus comes, darkness will flee and light will come. Therefore, since the day is almost here, we must remove the deeds of darkness like dirty old clothes and put on the armor of light.

1 Thessalonians 5:8
But let us who live in the light be clearheaded, protected by the armor of faith and love, and wearing as our helmet the confidence of our salvation.

Paul sums up chapter thirteen with the admonition to put away the sins of the night. Instead we must clothe ourselves with the presence of the Lord Jesus Christ.

Mark 13:34–37
"The coming of the Son of Man can be illustrated by the story of a man going on a long trip. When he left home, he gave each of his slaves instructions about the work they were to do, and he told the gatekeeper to watch for his return. You, too, must keep watch! For you don't know when the master of the household will return in the evening, at midnight, before dawn, or at daybreak. Don't let him find you sleeping when he arrives without warning. I say to you what I say to everyone: Watch for him!"

Wild parties are an occasion for excessive eating or drinking which leads to debauchery and drunkenness. Next is sexual promiscuity and immoral living. The difference between the two is promiscuity would refer to fornication or adultery, immoral living is to abandon oneself to unrestrained sexual activity. Lastly, quarreling which is a bitter disagreement that leads to harm. Jealousy is a greedy longing for something which belongs to another. This always is accompanied with the desire to take what others have by force.

Ephesians 5:8–9
For once you were full of darkness, but now you have light from the Lord. So live as people of light! For this light within you produces only what is good and right and true.

Instead, put on the presence of the Lord and stop thinking about yourself and ways to indulge your desires. Stop being selfish and wanting what you cannot have. God supplies all our needs, so stop trying to do it in your own strength.

Galatians 3:27
And all who have been united with Christ in baptism have put on Christ, like putting on new clothes.

Ephesians 6:13–17
Therefore, put on every piece of God's armor so you will be able to resist the enemy in the time of evil. Then after the battle you will still be standing firm. Stand your ground, putting on the belt of truth and the body armor of God's righteousness. For shoes, put on the peace that

comes from the Good News so that you will be fully prepared. In addition to all of these, hold up the shield of faith to stop the fiery arrows of the devil. Put on salvation as your helmet, and take the sword of the Spirit, which is the word of God.

Each Sunday as I get ready for church. I look through my closet and intentionally pick out some clothes to wear that day. Then I put them on one article at a time. It is intentional, we must intentionally put on the presence of God each morning to begin our day. Let's get dressed and ready to go!

Chapter 21

Rules for Food and Festivals

Romans 14:1–4
Accept other believers who are weak in faith, and don't argue with them about what they think is right or wrong. For instance, one person believes it's all right to eat anything. But another believer with a sensitive conscience will eat only vegetables. Those who feel free to eat anything must not look down on those who don't. And those who don't eat certain foods must not condemn those who do, for God has accepted them. Who are you to condemn someone else's servants? Their own master will judge whether they stand or fall. And with the Lord's help, they will stand and receive his approval.

Christians are at different levels of spiritual maturity. They also have diverse backgrounds that color their attitudes and practices. The first lesson to learn in living harmoniously with other Christians, therefore, is to stop judging others. We are to accept believers whose faith is weak and not to argue with them about what they think is wrong or right.

In my experience as a pastor of more than forty years in ministry, I have rarely seen anyone who can restrain themselves from judging and correcting a new Christian. I must admit I have been guilty of it a time or two myself.

Foods

Romans 14:2–3
For instance, one person believes it's all right to eat anything. But another believer with a sensitive conscience will eat only vegetables. Those who feel free to eat anything must not look down on those who don't. And those who don't eat certain foods must not condemn those who do, for God has accepted them.

One area of differing beliefs pertains to food, the eating of meat. One man's faith allows him to eat everything, but another man, whose faith is weak, eats only vegetables. The reason some Christians then were vegetarians is not stated. Since the issue is related to their Christian faith, it could be to insure against eating meat offered to idols which God had commanded them not to eat.

In, this situation neither believer should judge the other, look down on or despise the other for his belief. God has accepted both people and their faith. Therefore, we are not to judge each other on food.

We are all God's servants and no one has the right to judge or condemn another person's servant. It is God's right to judge our faith in these matters. So, we must not argue about our beliefs about what foods we should or should not eat.

Acts 15:19-20
"And so my judgment is that we should not make it difficult for the Gentiles who are turning to God. Instead, we should write and tell them to abstain from eating food offered to idols, from sexual immorality, from eating the meat of strangled animals, and from consuming blood.

This verse is most likely is where the issue comes from. The Gentiles could eat foods forbidden to the Jews but still were required not to eat foods where sin and immorality were involved. Leviticus states why they must not eat food from animals which have been strangled.

Leviticus 17:13-14
"And if any native Israelite or foreigner living among you

goes hunting and kills an animal or bird that is approved for eating, he must drain its blood and cover it with earth. The life of every creature is in its blood. That is why I have said to the people of Israel, 'You must never eat or drink blood, for the life of any creature is in its blood.' So whoever consumes blood will be cut off from the community.

Strangled by its definition means that it was not bled to death, letting the blood drain out of the meat. God made it clear in the Scriptures that no one was to eat blood. And even gave clear orders on how a person should kill an animal so that its meat could be consumed.

1 Corinthians 8:4–7
So, what about eating meat that has been offered to idols? Well, we all know that an idol is not really a god and that there is only one God. There may be so-called gods both in heaven and on earth, and some people actually worship many gods and many lords. But for us, There is one God, the Father, by whom all things were created, and for whom we live. And there is one Lord, Jesus Christ, through whom all things were created, and through whom we live. However, not all believers know this. Some are accustomed to thinking of idols as being real, so when they eat food that has been offered to idols, they think of it as the worship of real gods, and their weak consciences are violated.

Food offered to idols is not prohibited, yet it depends on a persons belief about the idol itself. Paul states, "some are accustomed to thinking of idols as real." This belief that idols are real would certainly lead someone to abstain from those foods.

Special Days

Romans 14:5–9
In the same way, some think one day is more holy than another day, while others think every day is alike. You should each be fully convinced that whichever day you choose is acceptable. Those who worship the Lord on a special day do it to honor him. Those who eat any kind of food do so to honor the Lord, since they give thanks to God before eating. And those who refuse to eat certain foods also want to please the Lord and give thanks to God. For we don't live for ourselves or die for ourselves. If we live, it's to honor the Lord. And if we die, it's to honor the Lord. So, whether we live or die, we belong to the Lord. Christ died and rose again for this very purpose—to be Lord both living and of the dead.

A second area of differing opinions was the significance of special days. One man considers one day more sacred than another; another man considers every day alike.

Colossians 2:16–17
So don't let anyone condemn you for what you eat or drink, or for not celebrating certain holy days or new moon ceremonies or Sabbaths. For these rules are only shadows of the reality yet to come. And Christ himself is that reality.

His concern was that each one should be fully convinced in his own mind, examining his heart to be sure he is doing what he feels the Lord would have him do. Over the last several years there has been a resurgence of Messianic Judaism, where there is a mixture of Christian faith in Jesus as Messiah and elements of Jewish traditions and the keeping of feasts. Personally, I don't understand this especially after all we have learned in Romans about not mixing law and grace. But, I must not judge even though I don't see the purpose of it.

Romans 14:8–13
If we live, it's to honor the Lord. And if we die, it's to honor the Lord. So whether we live or die, we belong to the Lord. Christ died and rose again for this very purpose to be Lord both of the living and of the dead. So why do you condemn another believer? Why do you look down on another believer? Remember, we will all stand before the judgment seat of God. For the Scriptures say,

> "As surely as I live,' says the LORD,
> 'every knee will bend to me, and every tongue will declare allegiance praise God."

Yes, each of us will give a personal account to God. So let's stop condemning each other. Decide instead to live in such a way that you will not cause another believer to stumble and fall.

Everything belongs to God, so, if we live it is to honor God and if we die we belong to God. Each of us will give an account of ourselves not our neighbor. Therefore, let's not condemn each other and decide to live in a way that will not cause another Christian to stumble and fall due to his convictions.

Romans 14:14–19
I know and am convinced on the authority of the Lord Jesus that no food, in and of itself, is wrong to eat. But if someone believes it is wrong, then for that person it is wrong. And if another believer is distressed by what you eat, you are not acting in love if you eat it. Don't let your eating ruin someone for whom Christ died. Then you will not be criticized for doing something you believe is good. For the Kingdom of God is not a matter of what we eat or drink, but of living a life of goodness and peace and joy in the Holy Spirit. If you serve Christ with this attitude, you will please God, and others will approve of you, too. So then, let us aim for harmony in the church and try to build each other up.

If someone believes eating meat is wrong, then for that person it is wrong. Another person may believe it's good to eat meat, to them it's right. The point is don't allow your freedom to destroy the conscience of someone who doesn't have the same freedom you do.

I was taught early in my faith that if what I ate offended someone I was to never eat that food again. This is certainly not what Paul is saying. Eating meat in front of someone who can't eat meat could make them feel condemned. So, in that case, don't eat meat in front of them. It doesn't mean you can never eat meat again. I would think, at this point, some of the readers are thinking about alcohol. The same principle applies with alcohol also.

The Kingdom of God is not about what we eat or drink. This is not a topic in which believers should spend time in debate and argument. The Kingdom of God is about living a life of goodness, peace and joy in the Holy Spirit.

If we have this attitude, God and people will be pleased. Our goal is to live in harmony with each other, encouraging and building each other up.

Eating without Faith is Sin

Romans 14:20–23
Don't tear apart the work of God over what you eat. Remember, all foods are acceptable, but it is wrong to eat

something if it makes another person stumble. It is better not to eat meat or drink wine or do anything else if it might cause another believer to stumble. You may believe there's nothing wrong with what you are doing, but keep it between yourself and God. Blessed are those who don't feel guilty for doing something they have decided is right. But if you have doubts about whether you should eat something, you are sinning if you go ahead and do it. For you are not following your convictions. If you do anything you believe is not right, you are sinning.

Personal convictions in areas where different views exist, Paul concludes, that whatever you believe about these things should be kept between yourself and God. A Christian must not insist on influencing a believer with different view to change his ways. Don't attack each other in these areas and cause your fellow believer to sin.

1 Corinthians 10:23
You say, "I am allowed to do anything" but not everything is good for you. You say, "I am allowed to do anything" but not everything is beneficial.

We may have freedom in an area but it might be better to abstain while around the person who believes differently. It may be allowed for me but not beneficial for the other person.

It all comes down to faith, what we believe about the

issue. Some people's freedom may have been another person's addiction. We must respect the convictions of people's faith. If a person's conviction says they cannot eat, then for them it is sin. We must never be a party to causing someone to fall into something God has set them free from. Respect each other's faith.

Chapter 22

Live in Harmony

Romans 15:1–4
We who are strong must be considerate of those who are sensitive about things like this. We must not just please ourselves. We should help others do what is right and build them up in the Lord. For even Christ didn't live to please himself. As the Scriptures say, "The insults of those who insult you, O God, have fallen on me." Such things were written in the Scriptures long ago to teach us. And the Scriptures give us hope and encouragement as we wait patiently for God's promises to be fulfilled.

We are still on the topic from chapter fourteen. Weak

faith was the issue regarding eating meat or vegetables. Now Paul speaks to the strong. They must be considerate and sensitive about these things, and not just do things to please ourselves. Our attitude is to honor and love each other, doing right and building each other up. Jesus didn't live to please himself, neither should we.

Live in Harmony

Romans 15:5–6
May God, who gives this patience and encouragement, help you live in complete harmony with each other, as is fitting for followers of Christ Jesus. Then all of you can join together with one voice, giving praise and glory to God, the Father of our Lord Jesus Christ.

Paul instructed us four times in Romans to live in harmony. To honor each other above ourselves and respect differing views from our own. We are under obligations to others, and it is therefore, our duty to please and to serve people.

Colossians 3:14
Above all, clothe yourselves with love, which binds us all together in perfect harmony.

1 Corinthians 1:10
I appeal to you, dear brothers and sisters, by the authority of our Lord Jesus Christ, to live in harmony with each

other. Let there be no divisions in the church. Rather, be of one mind, united in thought and purpose.

The word harmony means to "think the same." Our context is arguing with one another over foods and special days. We are not to condemn someone whose faith is weaker in regards to these issues. In this topic, we must all think the same, be in harmony with one another.

Accept Each Other

Romans 15:7–12
Therefore, accept each other just as Christ has accepted you so that God will be given glory. Remember that Christ came as a servant to the Jews to show that God is true to the promises he made to their ancestors. He also came so that the Gentiles might give glory to God for his mercies to them. That is what the psalmist meant when he wrote: "For this, I will praise you among the Gentiles; I will sing praises to your name." And in another place it is written, "Rejoice with his people, you Gentiles." And yet again, "Praise the LORD, all you Gentiles. Praise him, all you people of the earth." And in another place Isaiah said, "The heir to David's throne will come, and he will rule over the Gentiles. They will place their hope on him."

Jesus is our example of how we are to accept one another. We are reminded that Jesus came as a servant to the Jews. Therefore, we must live in harmony and in so doing bring glory to God.

Paul shares quotes from the Old Testament which call attention to the fact that the inclusion of the Gentiles in the Kingdom of God is not new promise from God. There were numerous scriptures which detailed God's plan to bring the Gentiles into the Kingdom of God.

Romans 15:13
I pray that God, the source of hope, will fill you completely with joy and peace because you trust in him. Then you will overflow with confident hope through the power of the Holy Spirit.

How we experience joy and peace is through trusting in God. The more we trust God, the greater our joy, the greater our peace, and the greater we experience this hope that the Bible elsewhere calls 'the anchor of the soul'. As we grow in grace, the Holy Spirit works within us, increasing the depth, the breadth and the intensity of that hope in our souls.

Paul's Reason for Writing

Romans 15:14–19
I am fully convinced, my dear brothers and sisters, that you are full of goodness. You know these things so well you can teach each other all about them. Even so, I have been bold enough to write about some of these points,

knowing that all you need is this reminder. For by God's grace, I am a special messenger from Christ Jesus to you Gentiles. I bring you the Good News so that I might present you as an acceptable offering to God, made holy by the Holy Spirit. So, I have reason to be enthusiastic about all Christ Jesus has done through me in my service to God. Yet I dare not boast about anything except what Christ has done through me, bringing the Gentiles to God by my message and by the way I worked among them. They were convinced by the power of miraculous signs and wonders and by the power of God's Spirit. In this way, I have fully presented the Good News of Christ from Jerusalem all the way to Illyricum.

Paul reminds them that he is a special messenger from Christ Jesus to the Gentiles. It seems at this point that Paul is wrapping up and preparing to finish his letter.

Romans 15:20–22
My ambition has always been to preach the Good News where the name of Christ has never been heard, rather than where a church has already been started by someone else. I have been following the plan spoken of in the Scriptures, where it says, "Those who have never been told about him will see, and those who have never heard of him will understand." In fact, my visit to you has been delayed so long because I have been preaching in these places.

Paul's ambition is to share the gospel with people which have never heard the message of Jesus. His delay in coming to Rome was caused by his preaching in place where the gospel has not yet reached.

Romans 15:23–29
But now I have finished my work in these regions, and after all these long years of waiting, I am eager to visit you. I am planning to go to Spain, and when I do, I will stop off in Rome. And after I have enjoyed your fellowship for a little while, you can provide for my journey. But before I come, I must go to Jerusalem to take a gift to the believers there. For you see, the believers in Macedonia and Achaia have eagerly taken up an offering for the poor among the believers in Jerusalem. They were glad to do this because they feel they owe a real debt to them. Since the Gentiles received the spiritual blessings of the Good News from the believers in Jerusalem, they feel the least they can do in return is to help them financially. As soon as I have delivered this money and completed this good deed of theirs, I will come to see you on my way to Spain. And I am sure that when I come, Christ will richly bless our time together.

Paul shares his plan to go to Spain to preach the gospel of Jesus. No one knows if Paul ever got to Spain, but we do know he did not go to Rome in the way he expected. Paul did make it to Rome but in chains.

Romans 15:30–33

Dear brothers and sisters, I urge you in the name of our Lord Jesus Christ to join in my struggle by praying to God for me. Do this because of your love for me, given to you by the Holy Spirit. Pray that I will be rescued from those in Judea who refuse to obey God. Pray also that the believers there will be willing to accept the donation I am taking to Jerusalem. Then, by the will of God, I will be able to come to you with a joyful heart, and we will be an encouragement to each other. And now may God, who gives us his peace, be with you all. Amen.

Paul encourages the Roman believers to join with him in the struggle of spreading the gospel. He asks for prayer to be rescued from those who refuse to obey God and for the generosity of believers, then he will come to Rome.

CHESTER GROSS

Chapter 23

Final Greetings

Romans 16:1–16

I commend to you our sister Phoebe, who is a deacon in the church in Cenchrea. Welcome her in the Lord as one who is worthy of honor among God's people. Help her in whatever she needs, for she has been helpful to many, and especially to me. Give my greetings to Priscilla and Aquila, my co-workers in the ministry of Christ Jesus. In fact, they once risked their lives for me. I am thankful to them, and so are all the Gentile churches. Also give my greetings to the church that meets in their home. Greet my dear friend Epenetus. He was the first person from the province of Asia to become a follower of Christ. Give my greetings to

Mary, who has worked so hard for your benefit. Greet Andronicus and Junia, my fellow Jews, who were in prison with me. They are highly respected among the apostles and became followers of Christ before I did. Greet Ampliatus, my dear friend in the Lord. Greet Urbanus, our co-worker in Christ, and my dear friend Stachys. Greet Apelles, a good man whom Christ approves. And give my greetings to the believers from the household of Aristobulus. Greet Herodion, my fellow Jew. Greet the Lord's people from the household of Narcissus. Give my greetings to Tryphena and Tryphosa, the Lord's workers, and to dear Persis, who has worked so hard for the Lord. Greet Rufus, whom the Lord picked out to be his very own; and also his dear mother, who has been a mother to me. Give my greetings to Asyncritus, Phlegon, Hermes, Patrobas, Hermas, and the brothers and sisters who meet with them. Give my greetings to Philologus, Julia, Nereus and his sister, and to Olympas and all the believers who meet with them. Greet each other with a sacred kiss. All the churches of Christ send you their greetings.

Phoebe (which means bright, radiant) was Paul's emissary to deliver this letter, so he wrote officially, I commend to you our sister Phoebe. The relationship mentioned is spiritual, not familial. Phoebe was a servant of the church in Cenchrea, a seaport a few miles east of Corinth. The word servant, is used for the office of deacon, Paul not only officially commended her, but also asked the Roman Christians to receive her in the Lord in a way worthy of the saints and to give her any help she may need from them. Paul explained, for that she has been a great help to many people, including himself. So they should help her since she had helped others.

Paul first met Priscilla and Aquila when he arrived in Corinth on his second missionary journey and worked with them at their trade of tentmaking. They had come to Corinth from Rome because of Claudius' decree that all Jews must leave Rome. They accompanied Paul when he left Corinth, but stayed in Ephesus when the group stopped briefly. There they ministered to Apollos and undoubtedly to Paul during his stay in Ephesus on his third journey, because they sent greetings to the Corinthian Christians. Shortly after that, they must have moved back to Rome and still later returned to Ephesus.

Paul continued with his greeting to numerous others, whom he had meet through his travels. Of all these individuals, only Priscilla and Aquila are mentioned elsewhere in the New Testament. Paul knew them all individually and sent personal greetings to them and their associates. Greet one another with a holy kiss, the mode of salutation like the handshake today. All the churches of Christ send greetings to you.

Final Appeal

Romans 16:17–20

And now I make one more appeal, my dear brothers and sisters. Watch out for people who cause divisions and upset people's faith by teaching things contrary to what you have been taught. Stay away from them. Such people are not serving Christ our Lord; they are serving their own personal interests. By smooth talk and glowing words, they deceive innocent people. But everyone knows that you are obedient to the Lord. This makes me very happy. I want you to be wise in doing right and to stay innocent of any wrong. The God of peace will soon crush Satan under your feet. May the grace of our Lord Jesus be with you.

Paul gave a final word of warning that they watch out for spiritual enemies: those who are divisive and seek to hinder the Lord's work. Believers are to keep away such false teachers, who were not serving Christ, but were slaves to their own desires. They were selfish gluttons. The problem, however, was that by smooth talk and flattery they deceived the minds of naive people.

Paul assured the Romans that he did not consider them naive. But he was concerned that they be wise about what is good, and innocent about what is evil. In Greek, it was used of wine that was not diluted and of metal that was not weakened in any way.

To conclude this warning Paul added the promise. The God of peace will soon crush Satan under your feet. False teachers were under Satan's influence, they would be destroyed and God would establish peace. Then Paul gave another benediction about God's grace. May the grace of the Lord Jesus be with you. Amen!

ABOUT THE AUTHOR

Chester is an author, pastor and church consultant. His contextual model of teaching has brought him to many nations. He is best known for his teaching on the Heart of the Father. Chester currently lives in Seattle, Washington.

Made in the USA
Columbia, SC
20 August 2017